D1283997

In the
Modern
Style

In the Modern Style

Building Furniture Inspired by the 20th-Century Tradition

The Taunton Press, Inc., 63 South Main Street, PO Box 5506, Newtown, CT 06470-5506

e-mail: tp@taunton.com

Distributed by Publishers Group West

Cover design: Susan Fazekas

Interior design: Susan Fazekas

Layout: Carol Petro

Library of Congress Cataloging-in-Publication Data:

In the modern style : building furniture inspired by the 20th-century
tradition / the editors of Fine woodworking.
       p. cm.
Includes bibliographical references.
   ISBN I-56158-581-5
 I. Furniture making. 2. House furnishings. I. Fine woodworking.
   TT194 .I52 2003
   684.I'04--dc2I
                                        2002009389

Printed in the United States of America

I0 9 8 7 6 5 4 3 2 I

The following manufacturers/names appearing in *In the Modern Style* are trademarks: Hettich International, Leigh, Masonite, Nicholson, 3M, Watco, and Wigglewood.

■ About Your Safety: Working with wood is inherently dangerous. Using hand or power tools improperly or ignoring safety practices can lead to permanent injury or even death. Don't try to perform operations you learn about here (or elsewhere) unless you're certain they are safe for you. If something about an operation doesn't feel right, don't do it. Look for another way. We want you to enjoy the craft, so please keep safety foremost in your mind whenever you're in the shop.

Special thanks to the authors, editors, art directors, copy editors, and other staff members of *Fine Woodworking* and *Home Furniture* who contributed to the development of the articles in this book.

CONTENTS

Introduction 2

PART ONE:

Style & Design 4

Table and Chairs with a Split Personality
E. E. "Skip" Benson 6

A Stylish Credenza
Patrick Warner 10

Extraordinary Built-ins
Ross Day 16

PART TWO:

Projects & Techniques 24

Component-Built Sideboard
Seth Janofsky 26

Build a Harvest Table
Gary Rogowski 38

Knockdown Computer Desk
David Tuttle 44

Building an Open-Pedestal Table
John Burchett 50

Frame-and-Panel Bed
David Fay 56

Mahogany Bedside Table
Charles Grivas 65

Curved Panels from a Vacuum Veneer Press
Mason Rapaport 73

A Hall Table That's Both Traditional
and Contemporary
Peter Korn 78

Entertainment Center in Quartersawn Maple
Peter Turner 84

Joinery for Light, Sturdy Coffee Table
Lindsay Suter 96

Shelving, Plain and Simple
M. Felix Marti 102

Gate-Leg Table Is Light but Sturdy
Gary Rogowski 106

Using Shop-Sawn Veneer
Paul Harrell 114

Strategies for Curved Work
Darryl Keil 124

PART THREE:

Inspiration 134

Dining Set in Cherry and Imbuya
Gene Martin 136

Audio Cabinet in Cherry and Wenge
Darrell Peart 138

Lacewood Writing Desk
Charles E. Johnson .142

Cloud Rise Bed
Gary Rogowski 144

Fresh Curves for a Kitchen Table
Michael Hurwitz 147

A Bent-Plywood Chair Built
for Good Posture
Gary Nakamoto 150

Circles, Inlays, and Curves Unite
a Bedroom Suite
Philip Ponvert 153

A Simple Table in Elm
Curt Wessel 156

Lacewood Stereo Cabinet
Peter Barrett 158

Contemporary Cherry Credenza
James Probst 160

Pearwood Cabinet on Stand
John Cameron 162

Contributors 164

Credits 167

Index 168

Some cabinetmakers work in well-established, historically defined furniture styles. Others can't help themselves when it comes to forging their own way, making furniture in their own style. The good designers among these mavericks pay some attention to history and to the great proportion found in nature, of course, but many can't resist the urge to go off in their own direction.

These woodworker/furniture designers are aided in their efforts to bend convention by using the latest materials and technology. Where historical woodworkers were limited by the tools available, today's artisans working in a contemporary motif are using lightweight manufactured woods, vacuum presses, steam boxes, and specially engineered glues to achieve their nontraditional ends.

As one of the woodworkers in this book says, "Furniture design is always a tussle over the fact that wood comes in straight, flat planks and yet is an organic and sensuous material."

Furniture makers working in the contemporary vein come down on the side of making the most of wood's sensuous and organic possibilities. As you look through the sections of this book you'll see that the safety net under these high-wire designers is their unstinting reliance on traditional proportion and a good eye to save them from failing.

The Taunton Press editors of this book assembled information from the pages of *Fine Woodworking* and *Home Furniture* magazines to help you explore this furniture frontier. Part One looks at the personality and artistic vision behind this approach. Part Two contains some projects and lots of training in the techniques that aid in their construction. Part Three includes inspirational examples made by some of the best artisans now practicing the woodworking craft. I hope that the ideas and information in this book help lift you on your own flight of furniture fancy.

—Tim Schreiner, publisher of *Fine Woodworking* and former editor of *Home Furniture*

Style & Design

Modern furniture is not so much a specific style as it is a mind-set, whereby the woodworker calls upon the best principles of other furniture styles to influence a design without imposing the restrictions that would otherwise be mandated. The result is furniture with a modern sensibility that complements today's lifestyles: furniture that is functional as well as beautiful with a unique character.

In this section you'll find woodworkers whose designs pay homage to their predecessors while finding new expressions for these principles—design principles that you can use for your own designs.

E. E. "SKIP" BENSON

Table and Chairs with a Split Personality

STYLE AND STRUCTURE.
Chairs and table reveal every-thing about the way they are put together and use their structure as ornament.

like things that reveal themselves slowly. It gives me a great deal of satisfaction when someone says that they have just discovered a shape or curve in a piece of my furniture after they have lived with it for several months or even years. These chairs and their table are full of details that speak in lowered tones. But they also raise a different, louder voice. I think they reflect a conversation between two sides of my design aesthetic and two sides of the material they're made from.

As I see it, furniture design is always a tussle over the fact that wood comes in straight, flat planks and yet is an organic and sensuous material. Similarly, my taste in furniture is two-sided. I'm interested in hard-edged, abstract furniture like Gerrit Rietveld's Zigzag chair, but I'm also drawn to furniture with softer, sinuous shapes. In these dining chairs and their table the rectilinear side is speaking louder, but the sinuous side is just as insistent. The chairs are four-square, comprised of major lines that are at first glance basically straight and perpendicular; yet there is not a completely straight line to be found.

LIGHTENING UP THE CUBE

Some years ago I made a set of a dozen chairs in acacia, big and squared off. At the time, I liked their heft. They were part of a group of dining room pieces that I designed in a Modernist mode, primarily composed of intersecting planes. As I looked back at my acacia chairs, however, they seemed to grow heavier by the month. And their unrelenting rectilinearity began to seem inhospitable. When I got a new commission for a set of dining chairs, I decided to revisit the four-square format, but to explore ways of softening the lines and edges and ways of attaining the same ruggedness, and the same strength, but without the leaden feeling.

OVER THE TOP. Designed for a family whose kitchen looks through the dining room to the outdoors, the chairs were kept low-backed to leave the view unobstructed.

Not long before this new commission came along I had made a side table with long legs and a thin top. I had 1-in.-thick stock, and instead of gluing up thick blanks to make the legs, I made the legs a sandwich separated by a reveal. This gave me rigidity with a light appearance. I used the same split-leg approach for these chairs, clamping the tenons of the arm rails and the side seat rails between the inner and outer halves of the legs.

Instead of dropping the slip seat directly into the frame of seat rails in the usual way, I elevated it an inch on three mid-rails whose ends I cut away at the top. By floating the seat this way I hoped to increase the sense of the chair's lightness.

SOFTENING THE SQUARE FORM

The treatment that I designed for the back slats was intended both to lighten and to soften the chair's appearance. I used curves on the top and bottom of each back slat to make the chair seem airy and to play off its harder edges. I also relieved the front faces of the slats to accept a sitter's back; the scooped section is widest on the top slat and narrowest on the bottom slat, forming a section of a cone that unifies the back.

To keep the legs from seeming post-like, I introduced, along with the split down the middle, a taper from top to bottom on the inside and outside faces of the legs. I then added two playful opposing curves at the floor. These little curves led me to think of this as the walking chair.

PLAYING GRAIN GAMES

The combination of flat and curved elements in these pieces gave me the opportunity to explore the difference in the appearance of wood when flatsawn and when quartersawn. That contrast can often be dramatic, as in the case of Douglas fir or as here, with white oak.

When cutting out parts I oriented the stock so that the narrow edges would show the linear grain and ray fleck of quartersawn figure and the wider sides would have the coarser, sometimes wilder flatsawn figure. With the flat-cut tops of the back posts and the many through-tenons, there was also plenty of room for displaying oak's

THESE LEGS ARE MADE FOR WALKING. The opposing curves at the bottom of the chair and table legs give them a sense of locomotion. The slip seat, raised on three mid-rails, seems ready to float away, too.

attractive end grain, and I burnished those surfaces to highlight it.

DETAILS

The unusually low-backed dining chairs are 30 in. high, 18 in. wide, and 17 in. deep; the extension dining table is 30 in. high, 42 in. wide, and 66 in. long when closed and 102 in. long with both leaves pulled out.

(opposite)
COMFORTABLE CUBES. Rigid geometry underlies Benson's chairs and table in white oak, but he softens it with curved and flared elements.

PATRICK WARNER

A Stylish Credenza

SYMMETRY AND SUBTLE SHADOW LINES give Patrick Warner's maple and yellow satinwood office credenza a dynamic visual rhythm. The same piece could serve as a buffet or as a case for audio and video equipment.

redenza, the Italian word for sideboard, has come to mean a low, lateral piece of office furniture for storage. I designed the credenza shown in the photo on the facing page for my office at home, and its dimensions and organization reflect that. It's fairly shallow because I couldn't afford to lose much floor space in my small office and because I don't like deep shelves—you can never get to the stuff at the back. Its top is counter height: I wanted to be able to work at it standing up sometimes. I chose sliding doors for the piece because of the tight quarters and because I like to roam around on my castered chair and don't need more obstacles. But part of the piece's beauty is that all these elements are adaptable to your own situation and so is the overall function of the piece.

OPTIONS AND ADAPTATIONS

Though I built my piece as a credenza, you could just as easily call it a buffet and use it in the dining room to store china and silverware. In that case, you might add a bank or two of drawers. And the doors, two or

A CASE AGAINST THE FINISH

It always bothers me when I begin applying the finish on a piece of furniture and suddenly realize I'm only halfway to completing the job. I work like crazy to apply good design, milling, and joinery to the furniture I make. That should be enough. Now just flood with Danish oil and deliver. Right? Well, perhaps. Danish oil is an easy, cheap, and often acceptable finish, but for furniture that will take a beating or for high-end work, a hard finish and some filling and coloring is often required. To obtain such a finish takes special skills, techniques and equipment, and often large amounts of time and money. This is not woodworking. It's chemistry, abrasives, coloring, compressors, spray guns, resins, solvents, clean rooms, and rubber gloves. And I'd rather not get tangled up in all of that if I can avoid it.

Finishes have their advantages, I admit. But when neither the environment nor the users are particularly threatening, a bare wood cabinet can be a refreshing change. Unfinished furniture is warmer both to the touch and the eye. It develops a nice patina and won't wear out a minute sooner

than work that's French polished or sprayed with automotive acrylic urethane. If it does suffer an occasional insulting hand smear or wet glass mark, a simple sanding or steel wool buff-up will quickly restore the original look. Try that with a catalyzed lacquer or an acrylic.

When you finish wood, you emphasize the grain, color, and figure, and this will limit its use in some applications. The soft, nonreflecting surfaces of unfinished wood, no matter the tree, play down the characteristics of the wood and put the material more in the service of the design.

A "no finish" finish is a natural with light woods like birch, beech, or maple that will yellow badly under finish. These are beautiful woods that shouldn't be discarded for this idiosyncrasy. Left unfinished, these woods yellow a little, but with the advance of the patina, the color mellows, bringing up light tans and other tonal subtleties, as you can see in the photo of the sliding door of my credenza at right.

If you're hesitant about making an unfinished piece for the house or a client, make something for the shop: perhaps a jig, fixture, or bench. Get firsthand experience with bare stock, and see

how it wears and ages. If you like it, think of how much more quality time you can invest in the next piece—time that would have been spent sanding, priming, sealing, and rubbing out that finish.

COMPLETE BUT UNFINISHED. Fed up with finishing, the author never flowed finish onto his credenza. Two years later, the maple and yellow satinwood have taken on the subtler tones time gives to bare wood.

three as you wish, could be mounted on hinges or pocket-door hardware.

You could also easily move the piece into a living room, and use it to house audio and video equipment. The center section could have a swiveling television slide installed, and a drawer or two could be added at the bottom of the side sections for tapes. In this arrangement, tambour doors would be an apt solution. They could be made as a pair that wrap laterally and meet in the middle or as three separate doors that track vertically.

If you wanted to use the cabinet as a display case, you could fit it with glazed doors, glass shelves, and, possibly, a glass top. In this arrangement, you might want to make shallow, traylike drawers, or simply install bottom-mount drawer slides on the shelving. And interior lighting also might be in order.

JOINERY DECISIONS

Once I'd resolved the configuration and dimensions of my credenza, I set to work on the anatomy—what the parts would be and how they would be joined. Whenever I build a piece for myself, I view it as an opportunity to experiment, so I tested a number of ideas in this credenza that had been brewing as I made furniture for less indulgent clients.

AROUND BACK. A half-lapped open frame is all the back the cabinet needs. It is tongued around its perimeter and glued into a groove in the carcase. The back affords excellent clamp access during glue-up.

I decided early on that the whole thing would be solid maple with a top and accents of yellow satinwood. I planned a fairly simple box carcase lifted off the ground by a separate and removable base. I hoped the base would lend the piece an airy feeling and avoid the impression of immovable weight that such office furniture often gives. I knew that the case inevitably would be dragged across a few floors, so I designed the base to be strong, though light, joining its legs and rails with dovetail tenons reinforced with machine-threaded knockdown fittings and hardwood corner braces, as shown in the drawing on the facing page.

For aesthetic reasons, I wanted the sliding doors in the same plane. So I left the center section of the case open to give the doors a space to slide into. I also decided to run the doors on a removable track. They would be installed with the track, avoiding the usual loose fit of sliding doors and the wide clearance required at the top to lift them out. The doors could be removed by unscrewing the track and sliding it out.

I chose a two-stage joinery method for the corners of the carcase. In the first stage, I joined the sides and subtop and bottom with tongue-and-groove joints across their full width. After the carcase was together, I routed out wedge-shaped recesses with a dovetail bit and filled them with yellow satinwood, as shown in the drawing. I make the recesses and the loose wedges with mating router templates. These floating wedges have the appearance of dovetails, and the joint is nearly as strong. I used the technique in a spirit of adventure to explore the decorative advantages it offered, and I certainly didn't exhaust them. You could also use any carcase joinery you like on this piece, from true dovetails or finger joints in solid wood to the range of possible joints in plywood or medium-density fiberboard.

I wanted to leave the back of the case largely open but give the piece resistance to racking stress. So I made a frame at the back of 2½-in.-wide members joined to each other with half-lap joints and to the case with a tongue and groove (see the photo at left).

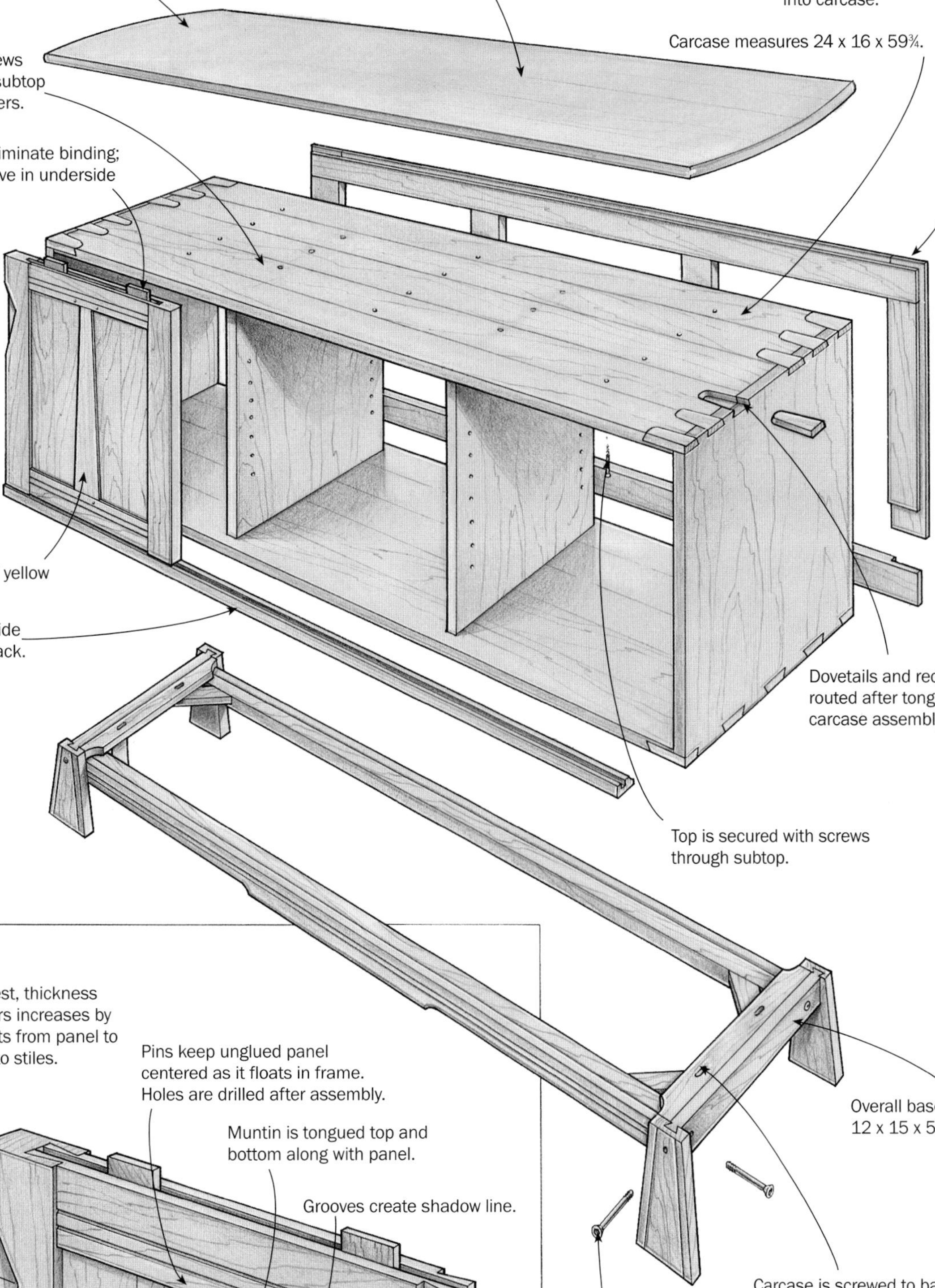

Ends of yellow satinwood top, arced at 8 ft. radius

Top measures $^{22}/_{32}$ x 16½ x 60½.

Back frame pieces are half-lapped together, then tongued into carcase.

Twin thread screws driven through subtop fix vertical dividers.

Carcase measures 24 x 16 x 59¾.

Shot runners eliminate binding; they run in groove in underside of subtop.

False muntin of yellow satinwood

Door runners slide in removable track.

Dovetails and recesses are routed after tongue-and-groove carcase assembly.

Top is secured with screws through subtop.

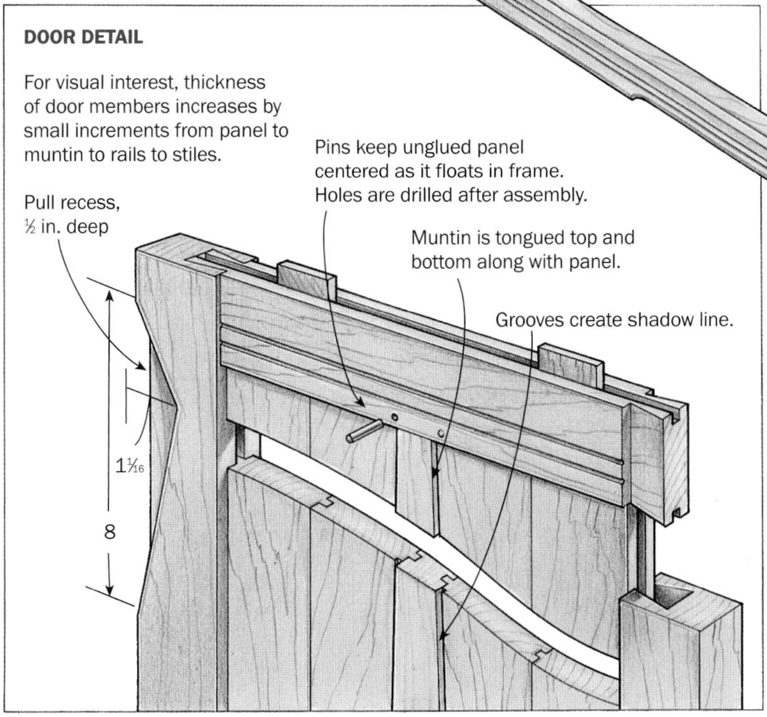

DOOR DETAIL

For visual interest, thickness of door members increases by small increments from panel to muntin to rails to stiles.

Pins keep unglued panel centered as it floats in frame. Holes are drilled after assembly.

Muntin is tongued top and bottom along with panel.

Pull recess, ½ in. deep

Grooves create shadow line.

Overall base dimensions: 12 x 15 x 58$^{13}/_{16}$

Carcase is screwed to base through ledger strip.

Cap screws engage threaded cross dowels.

$1^{1}/_{16}$

8

For the vertical dividers, I chose tongue-and-groove joints for the subtop and bottom with the tongues stopped so they wouldn't show at the front. There's no real glue surface on this joint, so I screwed the dividers in place with #10 twin-thread screws driven through the subtop and bottom. These wonderful screws contradict the old saw about not screwing into end grain: They get great purchase in a hardwood like maple.

When it came to the subtop and the bottom of the carcase, I looked for a way to make them that would simplify the glue-up. Instead of edge-joining them into panels and proceeding in the usual way with an increasingly frantic case assembly, I chose to install them as slats. I machined tongues and grooves along their edges and tongues on their ends and dadoed them to accept the tongues of the vertical dividers. When it came time to assemble, I first joined the sides, the back frame, and the rearmost slats of the subtop and bottom. Having only an open frame for a back greatly simplified the clamping. And once that initial assembly was clamped and squared up, I could then insert the rest of the slats at my leisure. A rare, tension-free glue-up.

The top went on when the case was finished. I made it of yellow satinwood and attached it with screws through the subtop.

DETAILS, DETAILS

With all the decisions made regarding configuration, dimensions, materials, and joinery, it might seem that the design process was at an end. But to me, one of the critical aspects of any piece of furniture is the detailing. Those subtle details are telling, particularly in a piece like this one that I had decided to leave unfinished (see the sidebar on p. 11). In a piece that's been filled or stained and lacquered, the grain and color of the wood can leap out at you and carry a plain design. But when the wood is left unfinished, it mellows and

recedes. I wasn't out to do anything startling, just to use what small devices I could to tie the piece together visually as well as structurally.

How thick is that?
You could make this credenza using ¾-in. material for nearly all the parts. In a dim room, it would be hard to tell yours from mine. But when light hit the two credenzas, they'd look quite different. I constantly play with thicknesses of material. Variations of as little as $\frac{1}{32}$ in. between adjacent boards can be perceived. I made the top and subtop each a shade under ¾ in. and did the same for the bottom and the door track. I made the sides $\frac{13}{16}$ in., so they didn't seem too skinny by comparison with the doubled elements at the top and bottom. I used 5/8 stock for the dividers to show that their structural role is subordinate to the sides. There are no strict rules governing the thicknesses of different elements, but if you play around with the size of parts, you'll find the overall appearance of the work can be subtly controlled.

Proud of it
Varying thickness is also useful in parts that are viewed face-on rather than from the edge. On the sliding doors, I made the stiles $\frac{1}{16}$ in. thicker than the rails, leaving them proud in the front. This slight variation in the plane of the door frames acknowledges the joint line and distinguishes the separate parts of the frame. I inset the panels $\frac{1}{16}$ in. from the rails to create a third plane. And at the center of the panels, I used a false muntin of yellow satinwood as an accent, which stands proud of the panel by a bit less than $\frac{1}{16}$ in. If these offsets were greater, the door might begin to seem fractured, but because they are only slight, they add visual nuance without attracting too much attention.

Shadow lines and shallow grooves

Shadows can be used like a pencil to vary the weight of the lines in a piece of furniture, to interrupt a featureless surface, or to outline and highlight a part or detail. As with the varying of thicknesses, the use of shadows can be overdone and requires careful control.

I created a reveal around the floating panels in the sliding doors to underscore the distinctness of the panel and the frame. The reveal is ¼ in. deep, and the shadows are dark. Shallower grooves cut to either side of the false muntins create a softer shadow and, therefore, mark the tapered shape with lighter emphasis. In the center section of the case, I created a shadow line with a chamfer at the back of the vertical divider where it meets the back frame. This balances the gap shadow between door and divider and picks out the divider as a discrete part (see the photo on p. 10).

The boldest shadow line in the credenza is the one between the bottom of the case and the front rail of the base. I dropped the rail to create this line, intending it to signify the functional separation between the carcase and the base. I've always liked the idea of making the base of a case piece look like a pedestal and tried to carry it out in this design. But I didn't want the two parts to be unrelated, and that led me to introduce several other details.

I had routed ⅛-in. grooves across the rails of the doors, and I echoed these on the base with the pair of grooves in the front rail. I hoped these grooves, with their lateral sweep across the length of the piece, would tie the three sections of the carcase together.

The leg design also was intended to relate the base to the carcase. I borrowed the tapered form from the false muntins and emphasized it (while breaking up the

ANGLED FORMS PLAY OFF STRAIGHT LINES. Floating dovetail wedges, tapered muntins, and recessed triangular handholds form a subtheme in Warner's rectilinear composition in lines and planes.

legs' blockiness) with grooves parallel to the tapered edges.

A curve or two for contrast

As I was finishing up, I saw that virtually all the lines in the credenza were rectilinear. Because the top was of contrasting material anyway, yellow satinwood to the maple of the base and carcase, I decided to express the distinction between them a little further by arcing the ends of the top and rounding over the edges. I cut the arc on an 8-ft. radius with a router and template and the roundover with a router and a ⅜-in. roundover bit. I used the same bit to round over the front edges of the shelves to give them a visual link to the top.

ROSS DAY

Extraordinary Built-ins

A few years ago, two women walked into my shop unannounced. One of them was the daughter of a client; the other was her interior designer. They were familiar with my furniture and asked whether I would consider making built-in cabinets for them. I said I was not doing cabinets anymore, just furniture. But the women said they didn't want cabinets in the traditional sense. They were looking for built-ins that looked like high-quality furniture.

My curiosity was piqued, because I had never done anything like this before. Case-good construction and furniture making really are two separate disciplines. Built-in cabinets generally are utilitarian in nature. To keep costs under control, the choice of materials and construction follow certain predictable paths. For one, doors often are attached with large European-style hinges, and drawers are usually set on metal slides, all of which make for easier adjustment and faster construction. Cabinets usually are attached to walls with screws, and moldings, if any, are nailed in place.

Fine furniture requires more handwork, such as hand-cut dovetail joints, which are time-consuming and costly if done on a large scale. But furniture presents the builder (and client) with many more options. The choices of materials are endless, and the design possibilities vast. These are all the reasons why I got into furniture making and why I took on this commission.

DESIGNING A BEDROOM FROM SCRATCH

My mission was to create a refuge—a place to relax, reflect, and re-energize. The homeowners are both avid readers and art collectors and demanded lots of storage and display space. Their wish list included an entertainment/display center, a corner cabinet, three sliding door screens, three large wardrobes, two bookcases, and even some freestanding furniture: a platform bed and two nightstands. Aesthetically, the clients were after what they called a "contemporary Asian feeling."

I looked for a traditional and historical link that I could update and found it in a book on Japanese architecture. I was intrigued by a style of fence and gate that utilized a latticework pattern with decora-

A UNIFYING THEME.
Latticework is used on all of the cabinet doors. Some intersecting members are pinned using brass, colored an antique brown.

tive nails at the joints. I sketched out various ideas and came up with a scaled-down version of this latticework pattern, which could be repeated throughout the room. The clients liked the idea. The latticework, which is applied to all of the door panels, became the focal point of many of the pieces, both large and small, and helped tie them all together visually.

TOP-QUALITY MATERIALS MAKE A DIFFERENCE

The clients requested that the primary wood be Japanese oak, a tight-grained, honey-colored wood. Unfortunately, it isn't available anymore. I was, however, able to track down some old-growth quartersawn American white oak and quartersawn French oak veneer. These are lighter in color and finer in grain than typical white oak and turned out to be a good match.

All of the boxes and panels were veneered medium-density fiberboard (MDF). Edges were covered with solid, shopmade banding, about ⅛ in. thick. Thicker edge-banding allowed me to ease the corners and provided a durable surface. I also used solid maple, primarily for drawer sides and backs. To keep shelves from sagging, I first built up a core of a ¾-in. plywood surfaced on both sides with ¼-in. MDF. Then I veneered the faces and finished off the shelves with ¾-in.-thick edge-banding.

The designer provided handmade pulls from India. But when I first saw them, I wasn't too thrilled. The pulls were coated with layers of lacquer, shielding highly polished brass. To soften the glare, I sandblasted the pulls and other hardware and chemically treated them to yield a more subtle, antique brown finish.

The designer also suggested using some fabrics as an accent. The door panels of the

FABRIC ADDS TEXTURE. The top of the corner cabinet is covered in straw matting. The same material is also applied to the soffit.

entertainment center were wrapped in silk, and the corner cabinet was adorned with straw matting. These fabrics added color and texture to the overall scheme.

JOINERY RANGED FROM BISCUITS TO HAND-CUT DOVETAILS

I used exposed joinery throughout. All of the rails and stiles were connected with bridle joints (also known as slip joints). The tops of lower cabinets (and nightstands) were veneered and framed with solid wood, then joined at the corner with bridle joints. The rails and stiles of the headboard were joined the same way.

All drawers have variable-spaced, hand-cut dovetails with narrow pins. The drawers were built upon frames (called NK drawers) that act as slides, in tandem with wooden guides. NK drawers are very strong, and because the drawer sides don't contact the case, drawers are easy to open and close.

The boxes themselves were fashioned like typical built-ins. Biscuits were used to join the cases, and the backs were glued into rabbets. But biscuits don't have a lot of holding power at the narrow ends. So I added dowel joints at the front corners of the cases to make sure they would stay tight. Side-by-side cases were connected to each other using joint-connector bolts, which I tinted antique brown to match the rest of the hardware.

TIME SPENT REFINING DETAILS PAYS OFF

The word "details" implies small or subordinate, but in furniture, details are as important as the materials, joinery, and overall design. Screw up the details, and the entire project is weaker as a result. Take shadow lines, for example. If a cabinet has too few, it looks bland; too many, and it takes on a busy look. On traditional doors, shadow lines typically are achieved through

FREESTANDING PIECES COMPLEMENT THE BUILT-INS. Similar exposed joinery and design details went into the nightstands and bed.

the use of raised panels and profiled rails and stiles. This project had none of those details; instead, I created shadow lines by varying the thickness of parts. For example, the rails are $\frac{3}{32}$ in. thinner than the stiles on all of the doors. The latticework on the flat panels is set back from the rails by another $\frac{3}{32}$ in. The valances that run atop all of the pieces are gapped, leaving a ¼-in. shadow line. Additionally, the bridle joints on the corners of the headboard, nightstand top, and a few other places are emphasized.

CARCASE CONSTRUCTION IS PRETTY STRAIGHTFORWARD. But lots of work went into the doors. Bridle joints are used on all of the rails and stiles. On the inside, sliding wire racks are used for storage.

HAND-CUT JOINTS AND HANDMADE PULLS FROM INDIA. All of the drawers have variably spaced, hand-cut dovetails. The author sandblasted the shiny original finish on the pulls, then patinated them antique brown.

Either the tenon is proud or the walls of the mortise protrude by a small amount.

The exposed-joinery concept was carried over to the latticework. Where members cross, I added diamond-shaped brass pins, which were patinated to match the rest of the hardware.

A NEW DISCIPLINE IS BORN

When it came time to deliver and install the cabinets, I remembered one of the reasons why I got out of cabinetmaking. This can be tough, dangerous work. It took three guys and a Genie Lift to get everything in place. We had to build a bridge over a sunken living room to make a platform big enough to get the lift in position. Then the cabinets took a slow, wobbly ride up 12 ft. before being pulled over the railing to the second floor. That each box made it safely into the room was a minor miracle.

All built-ins must be fitted to walls, which are never perfectly plumb nor flat. To fit these cabinets, I used scribe strips. The cabinets were held back approximately 3 in. to 4 in. from the walls, and the strips were handplaned to fill the gap. The method made fitting a lot easier and added another shadow line to the rather plain sides of the bookshelves and wardrobes.

This job would have been a lot harder to accomplish had I not been trained in both basic cabinetry and furniture making. For this challenging project, I drew on all of my skills, and that led me to a new standard of woodworking, somewhere in the great divide between case goods and fine furniture. I call this hybrid "cabineture," a style of working that combines the craftsmanship and ideals of both disciplines.

Although technically still a built-in, "cabineture" has its feet planted firmly in the traditions of fine furniture. Standard-quality cabinets lack the refinements of "cabineture."

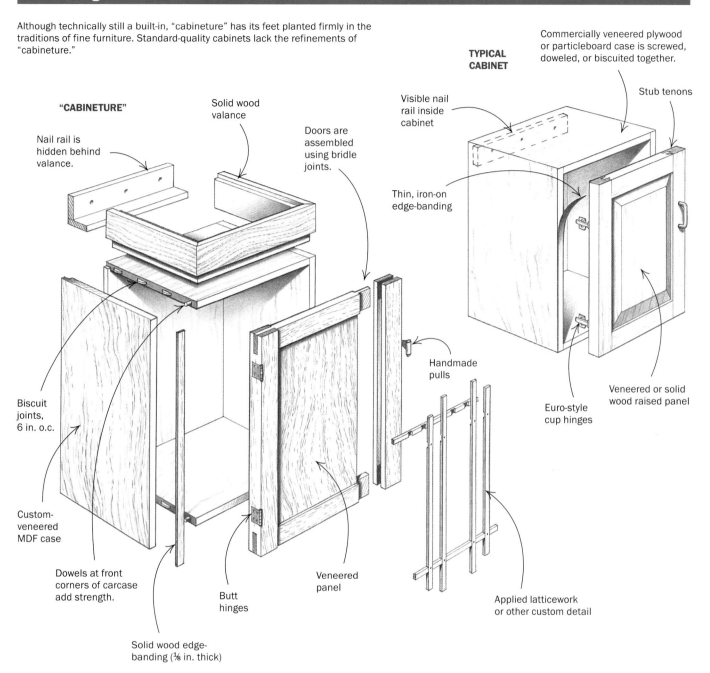

"CABINETURE"

Nail rail is hidden behind valance.

Solid wood valance

Doors are assembled using bridle joints.

Biscuit joints, 6 in. o.c.

Custom-veneered MDF case

Dowels at front corners of carcase add strength.

Butt hinges

Solid wood edge-banding (⅛ in. thick)

Veneered panel

Handmade pulls

TYPICAL CABINET

Commercially veneered plywood or particleboard case is screwed, doweled, or biscuited together.

Visible nail rail inside cabinet

Stub tenons

Thin, iron-on edge-banding

Veneered or solid wood raised panel

Euro-style cup hinges

Applied latticework or other custom detail

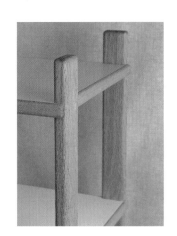

Projects & Techniques

Now that you've learned about the versatility of the modern style, we'll take a look at some creative projects. Whether you want to build a computer desk, a bedside table, or a frame-and-panel bed, you'll find what you're looking for in this section. You'll also learn some techniques common to modern furniture that allow you to manipulate wood in ways unheard of before the 20th century. You can apply these to the projects here or your own designs.

SETH JANOFSKY

Component-Built Sideboard

I work alone in a very small shop. Actually, in two small shops. My machines rub elbows in a cramped basement room, while my workbench and hand tools are up on the first floor in another small room. The two shops are not connected by a stair, and getting from the machines to the workbench requires a walk outside, uphill around the house. So one of the things I try to do when making furniture is design for efficient construction, breaking things down into subassemblies that I can handle easily in my small space and work on comfortably by myself. I also like the finished pieces of furniture to be as easy to handle, pack, and move as possible. I've developed ways of designing that take these things into account while still aiming to produce striking, useful pieces. The white oak sideboard I recently completed is a good example of the way I design to accommodate these various needs while bringing unity to a piece that, when finished, remains essentially a stack of separate components.

DESIGN TIME: COMPROMISE BEGETS GOOD FURNITURE

As odd as it may sound at first, I think the finest furniture is the result of a lot of compromise. Not the kind of compromise that leads to cutting corners and doing less than the best possible work, but rather the compromise that's involved when you strive to balance three things: the aesthetic needs of

Two Cases on a Base

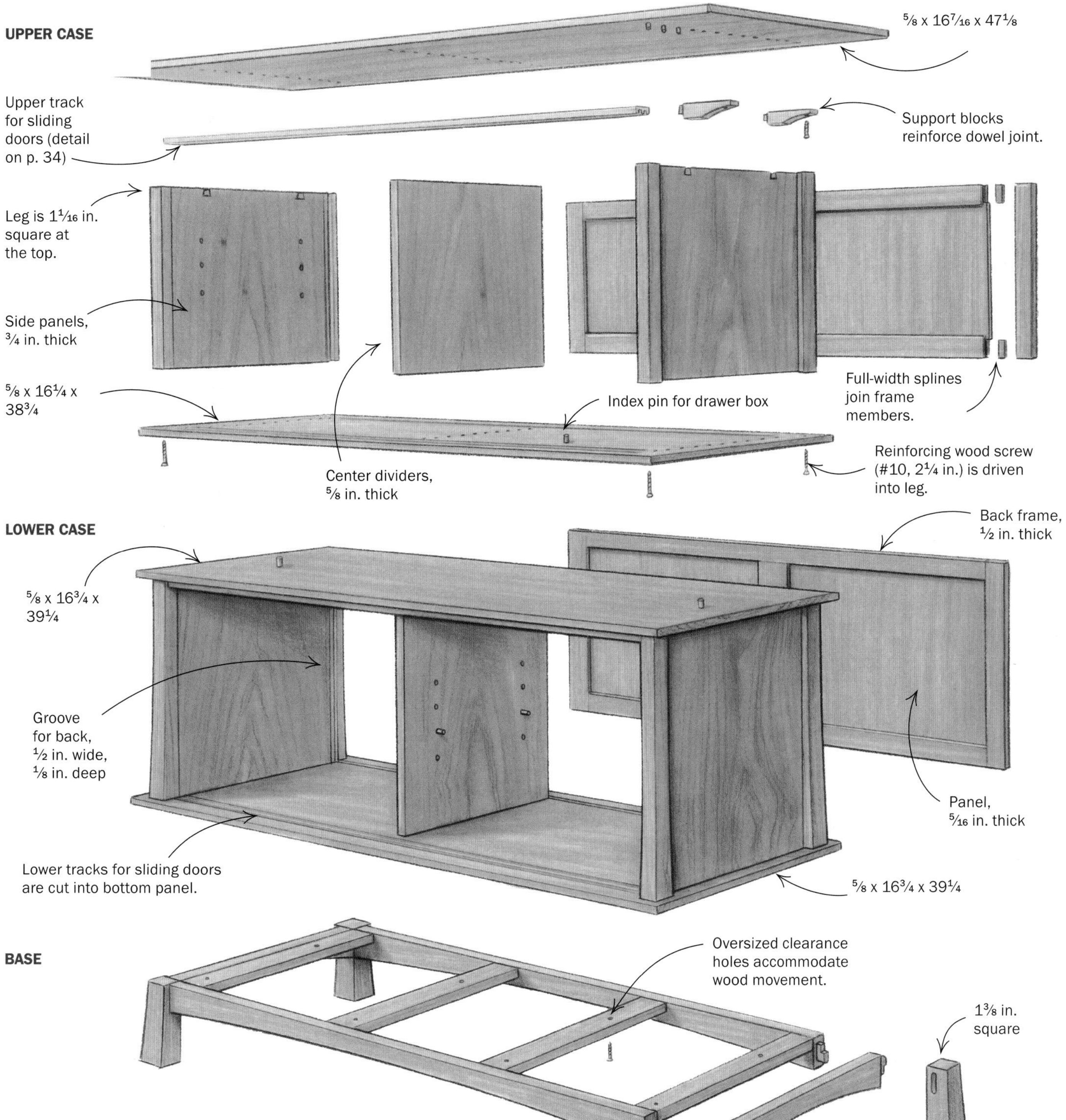

UPPER CASE

$5/8 \times 16^{7}/16 \times 47^{1}/8$

Upper track for sliding doors (detail on p. 34)

Support blocks reinforce dowel joint.

Leg is $1^{1}/16$ in. square at the top.

Side panels, $3/4$ in. thick

$5/8 \times 16^{1}/4 \times 38^{3}/4$

Index pin for drawer box

Center dividers, $5/8$ in. thick

Full-width splines join frame members.

Reinforcing wood screw (#10, $2^{1}/4$ in.) is driven into leg.

LOWER CASE

Back frame, $1/2$ in. thick

$5/8 \times 16^{3}/4 \times 39^{1}/4$

Groove for back, $1/2$ in. wide, $1/8$ in. deep

Panel, $5/16$ in. thick

Lower tracks for sliding doors are cut into bottom panel.

$5/8 \times 16^{3}/4 \times 39^{1}/4$

BASE

Oversized clearance holes accommodate wood movement.

$1^{3}/8$ in. square

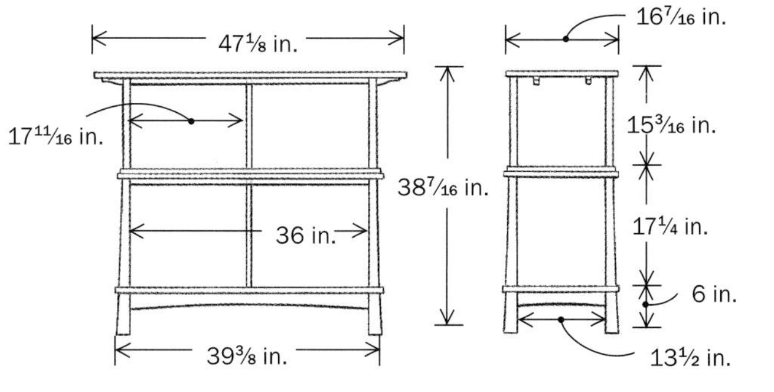

Loose tenons notched to cross at corners.

$1^{11}/16$ in. square

$47^{1}/8$ in.

$16^{7}/16$ in.

$17^{11}/16$ in.

36 in.

$39^{3}/8$ in.

$38^{7}/16$ in.

$15^{3}/16$ in.

$17^{1}/4$ in.

6 in.

$13^{1}/2$ in.

For convenience of construction, the sideboard is built in stacking components. The upper case is indexed on the lower one by a pair of pins, and it can be lifted off; the base is screwed to the lower case. All parts are solid wood. To avoid wood-movement problems, the grain is run vertically on end panels and center partitions and end-to-end on horizontal panels.

a piece, the requirements of function, and construction that is sound and efficient. There should be a back-and-forth between aesthetics, function, and construction during the design process; the craftsman has to see to it that all three purposes are well served and that none of the three dominates at the expense of the others. With skill and conscientious effort, and a little luck, the end result will be a piece of furniture that sits, as it were, at the best possible balance point of these three demands.

When I set out to make this sideboard, I had a number of considerations in mind. In terms of function, I wanted a useful piece with a serving surface, compartments for dishes, probably with some adjustable shelves, and drawers for silverware. I didn't want a piece that was limited to use as a sideboard, however. I wanted one that could also function as a display cabinet for pottery or for other decorative objects. Aesthetically, I had in mind something light and delicate-looking, even as it was strong and durable. Nothing flamboyant but rather a quiet, refined kind of thing. As for the specific style, I explored in the general direction of other cabinets I've made, which blend traditional Japanese and Scandinavian-modern influences. In terms of construction, I wanted solid, straight-forward joinery—structurally sound, efficient to make, subjugated to the quiet design I envisioned.

Legs and Sides Are First Laid Out and Cut

TEMPLATE WITH A BRAIN. Before bandsawing, the author traces the curve of the leg from a ¼-in.-thick MDF template. The template is also a story stick, marked with the locations of all of the horizontal elements in the sideboard.

CLEVER MEASUREMENT. The leg template itself is used to set the stop block for crosscutting the case sides and legs. When the template is removed, there is a gap beneath the stop block for sawdust relief.

DON'T MOVE THAT STOP BLOCK. After cutting the leg segments for the upper case, the author leaves the stop block where it is to cut the sides for the upper case.

Putting these factors together, I came up with a solid white oak sideboard that is, in its essence, simply two boxes on a base. To best use the beautiful wide boards I found, I opted for a solid wood structure, which is a hybrid of simple plank construction and post-and-panel construction. A top surface with long overhangs on both ends showcases the single-board top and establishes the visual tone of the piece. To give the separate boxes visual unity and to create a vertical sweep to balance the strong horizontal line of the top, I designed curved legs that extend up through the piece. The legs have a powerful impact both on the aesthetics of the sideboard and on the method of construction. They provide just one example among many of how an aesthetic decision dictates to the technical, and how the technical responds to the aesthetic and exerts its influence. Likewise with the functional requirements—back and forth, as the design comes together.

LEGS AND SIDES MADE AS A UNIT

The success of the sideboard depended on getting the legs and sides just right; I needed to create a convincing sense of continuity up the sides to make the components of the sideboard read as a unified piece. To get the best possible continuity of grain and color and curvature, I decided to make the legs

Then They Are Splined and Glued

LEGS: THE HEART OF THE DESIGN. To bring visual unity to a sideboard composed of stacked components, the author designed legs that carry through the cases and the base. He achieves continuity of grain and color by shaping the legs and the side panels as full-height pieces and cutting them apart. Where horizontal members interrupt the flow, he removes a matching amount of material from the legs and sides.

SPECIAL CAULS, KERFED AND CORKED. For gluing the legs to the case sides, the author makes kerfed cauls that conform to the curve of the legs. A layer of cork on the unkerfed edge protects the workpiece.

and the side panels full length, mark them carefully, do most of the machining and sanding, and only then cut them apart into segments. It was necessary to think of and work on the legs and side panels as a unit.

When I had sorted the wood for the project and laid out the basic parts, I began cutting and shaping the legs and preparing the side panels. After initial milling of the pieces, I cut the two side panels to exact width (but leaving them long) and put them aside. I made a full-sized template of the leg out of medium-density fiberboard (MDF) and marked it with the cabinet divisions so that it could be used as a story stick. Then I cut the leg blanks to length, traced the outer curve off the template, and bandsawed them to rough shape. I clamped all four legs together on the top of the table saw and quickly smoothed the curve, first with a belt sander, then with a random-orbit sander. This is perhaps a somewhat inelegant method, but it brought the legs to a smooth, uniform curve very quickly. I touched up each leg individually with a block plane and scraper and finished by chamfering the edges with the block plane and sanding block. All of this was done before cutting the legs into their segments to ensure that when the sideboard was finished, each leg would read as one uninterrupted, flowing curve, despite the divisions in it.

I had marked the sides and the legs carefully to preserve the orientation of all of the parts after they were cut into segments. Then I began the cutting. Using a crosscut sled on the table saw, I cut the legs and sides into their component parts. I set the stop blocks for these cuts directly from the marks on the leg template. Before leaving the table saw, I also cut grooves in the legs and sides for the splines that would align the parts during glue-up. Also, with a ½-in. dado set, I cut grooves in the rear legs for the case backs.

Before I could glue the legs to the side panels to make the completed case sides, I had to drill dowel holes in the side panels and prefinish the legs and panels (these processes are described in the sidebars on pp. 28–29). Also, to solve the problem of clamping curved legs, I made a set of kerfed, cork-faced softwood cauls that would conform to the gentle curve of the legs under clamping pressure. As I glued up, the splines kept the sides and legs in plane, but I had to check carefully during the clamping to make sure I kept the end-to-end alignment of the parts exact.

DOWELING: A GREAT PLACE FOR THINGS TO GO WRONG

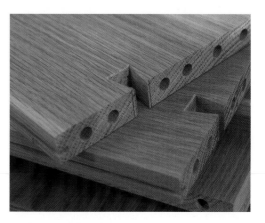

I often use dowels in carcase joinery. I prefer to use concealed joinery on many of the pieces I build, and dowel joints are straightforward to make and structurally sound. But I don't much like the actual work of doweling. It's nerve-racking, and there's a lot of potential to botch things at this stage, especially when there are many parts involved and many holes to drill, with a lot of careful alignment to be kept. To counter the tendency to lose track of what holes need to be drilled where, I take the time to set things up very carefully indeed.

The job begins with making doweling jigs, new ones for each piece of furniture. The jigs are simply pieces of hardwood cut to the length of the joint to be made and sized to the thickness of the parts to be joined. The jigs don't take long to make, but I take care to make them precisely—a precise jig will save a lot of time and trouble. I drill the guide holes carefully at the drill press. Each jig has a block of wood at the back to reference it off of the back edge of the workpieces, keeping everything in alignment. For this sideboard I also needed a few spacers to locate the jigs properly when I was joining parts of differing widths. For the basic joinery in the sideboard, I made two jigs: one ¾-in.-thick jig for the case sides and one ⅝-in.-thick jig for the center partitions, to match the thickness of these components. Each vertical-to-horizontal joint in this sideboard has 12 to 14 ⁵⁄₁₆-in. dowels spaced on approximately 1-in. centers. I chose a dowel diameter slightly on the small side to reduce the risk of corrugating the outside of the panels, which can be caused by dowel expansion and hydraulic pressure from the glue if the dowels are too close to the outer surface.

For setting the jigs on the horizontal parts with maximum accuracy, I made a ¼-in. plywood spacer sized exactly to the interior width of the sideboard. I marked the precise centerline of the spacer and marked centerlines on all of the horizontal parts. This enabled me to locate the doweling jigs accurately and easily even though the horizontal parts were all left long at the time of doweling. I wanted them long so that I could dry-assemble the cases and look at them before deciding how long the various setbacks and overhangs should be.

Drilling the dowel holes took an entire day, the first part of it given over to making sure everything was properly prepared, clearly marked, at hand, and thoroughly thought through. Then I spent about eight hours anxiously checking, double-checking, and finally drilling some 320 holes.

The fit of the dowels in the holes is very critical in glue-ups with this many dowels (80 in each box); a bit too tight and it may be impossible to pull the joints together even with all of the clamps in the shop. In this case I ended up shaving all 160 dowels with a handplane to get them just right. Also, because of the time involved in actually applying the glue and getting the joints together, I glued each case in two separate operations; first gluing the sides to the bottom, then to the top.

I have considerable faith in the integrity of dowel joinery, but still I decided to reinforce the cases at each corner with a long wood screw driven into the center of each leg. These screws were insurance against mishandling of the sideboard. It's always possible someone might try to carry this

■ Dowel Duty

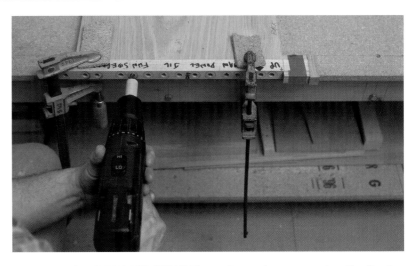

REGISTRATION, QUICK AND CLEAN. The author makes custom doweling jigs for each new piece he builds. He sizes the jigs to the thickness of the stock so they are automatically in proper alignment when clamped to the workpiece. He uses a pair of shopmade depth stops, one for end-drilling and a longer one for the shallower face-drilling. A level in the drill body helps him keep the drill horizontal.

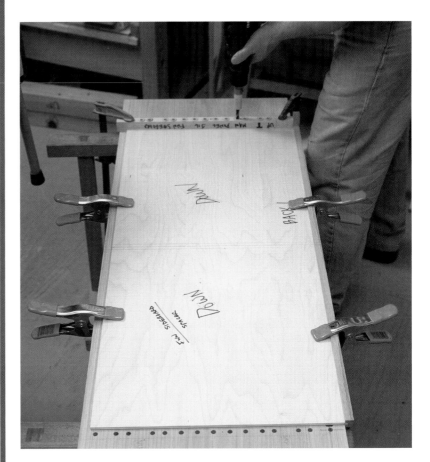

GUIDE BOARD ELIMINATES LAYOUT. With their varying setbacks and overhangs, the horizontals in the sideboard differ in length. But the author can dowel them all with the same template because it works off a centerline registration mark. A strip of wood tacked to one long edge of the template serves as a stop.

sideboard away by its overhanging top, perhaps even full of heavy dishes. At the top I used a different method of reinforcement. Screws weren't appropriate there because even if the holes were carefully plugged with tapered face-grain plugs, they would have interrupted the pristine top surface. So instead I made a pair of supports for each end of the top. These supports are glued and screwed to the underside of the top and dovetailed into the case sides, mechanically locking the top to the sides.

FINISH BEFORE REACHING THE END

I begin applying finish as the parts of a piece are made, before the gluing together starts—sometimes even before the parts are completed. Although it is a little time-consuming at certain stages of the work, this method saves time in the long run by making errant glue so easy to clean up (see the sidebar below). Not all surfaces need to be prefinished—just those that are involved in gluing operations or those that will be

difficult to finish after assembly. I tape the glue-joint areas before applying finish.

I use only two types of finish for fine furniture: oil finishes (usually a Danish oil) and shellac, both with an overcoat of wax. Either is suitable for use on white oak, but I think the padded-on shellac finish—sort of a French polish but without the intent to fill the pores fully and without the technique associated with that aim—is the more delicate of the two methods, so that's what I chose. For nearly all of the parts of this piece, I used two coats of padded-on shellac. The exceptions were the Port Orford cedar door panels, which required more, and the top surface of the sideboard, which, for durability in use, got a sealer coat of shellac and then several coats of oil. The visible end-grain areas generally needed an extra coat or two of shellac and some extra polishing between coats. When the shellacking was completed, I applied an overcoat of furniture wax and buffed up the sheen I wanted—a little, but not too much.

And now for my appalling confession: Despite being skilled with a handplane, I

■ Prefinish Before Glue-Up

TAPE IT OFF AND FINISH IT UP. Finish is applied to some parts before assembly to make glue cleanup easier. Areas that will receive glue are taped off.

COMPONENT CONSTRUCTION GREATLY SIMPLIFIES ASSEMBLY. Instead of one big, unwieldy, hair-raising glue-up, there are four smaller ones: two cases, one base, and one drawer box.

rely heavily on the use of a random-orbit sander to prepare wood for finishing and even between coats of finish. It simply is faster when there's a lot of work to do. I reach for the handplane whenever it looks as though I can get a job done quicker and better that way, but most surfaces get sanded with the random-orbit sander.

At the start of this sideboard job, I had the panels thicknessed by a wide belt sander, so now I could start the random-orbit sanding at 180 grit. I followed that with 320 grit. I used the random-orbit machine even after I'd begun applying the finish, knocking down each coat of shellac with progressively more worn 320-grit discs until I had the fine finish I wanted. On smaller parts I often sand by hand, but it's necessary to go to 400 or 600 grit and sometimes the finest steel wool to get a finish equivalent to the one produced by the sander at 320 grit.

I drilled the holes for the shelf pins after the parts were completely finished. To get a very clean, polished, slight chamfer around the rim of each hole, I used a pointed aluminum-oxide grinding tip in my cordless drill instead of a countersink bit.

THE BASE: EXPEDIENT SUPPORT

My original sketches of the sideboard (see the drawing below) showed feet tenoned directly into the bottom of the lower case. But as soon as I looked at my mock-up, I could see that the piece would require some additional support underneath. I decided to make a base that was a separate structure screwed to the underside of the lower 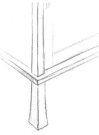 case. It seemed to me that a little additional mass below would be desirable from an aesthetic point of view as well. To link the base visually with the case above, I bandsawed an arch along the bottom edge of the rails, echoing the curve of the legs. The rails are fairly thick, and cross braces between the front and back rails, directly under the cen-

Base Basics

SLIM BUT STRONG. To make a strong base without wide rails, the author made the rails $^{15}/_{16}$ in. thick, added cross braces, and notched the spline tenons for deeper penetration into the legs.

ter of each compartment, give additional support.

The base was assembled with spline-tenon joinery, a strong, simple method that allowed me to build the whole base in a couple of hours (see the photos above). With spline tenons, all of the parts can be cut to exact length on the table saw. This makes for great accuracy, and the construction is very expedient, with no tenon shoulders to cut and adjust. I cut all of the mortises on a horizontal mortising machine using a single setup.

To avoid an awkward look in the finished legs, I planed a very slight curve on the two inside faces of each foot to echo the more pronounced sweep of the two outer faces. This is a fine point, but it lightened the stance of the sideboard noticeably.

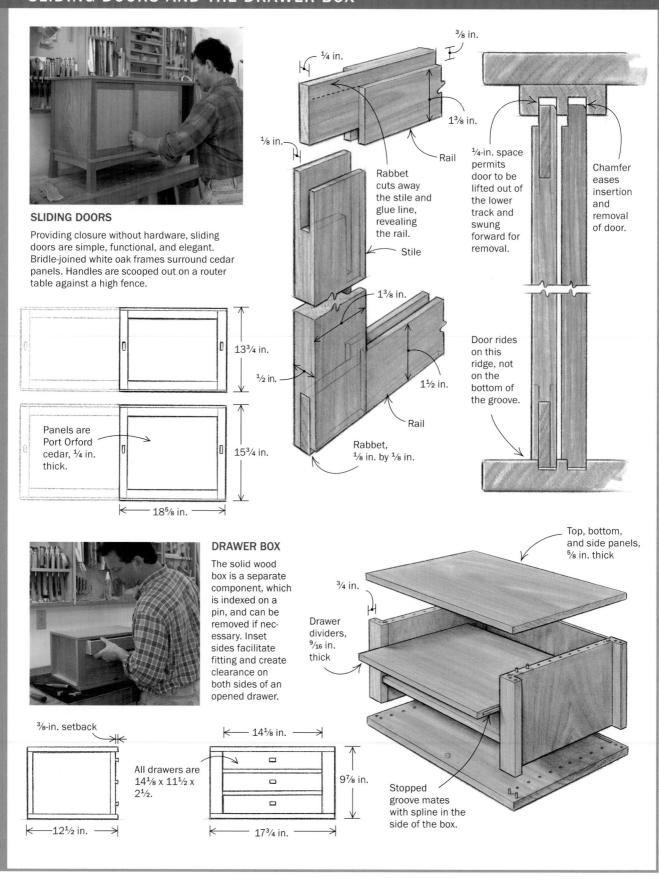

SLIDING DOORS

Providing closure without hardware, sliding doors are simple, functional, and elegant. Bridle-joined white oak frames surround cedar panels. Handles are scooped out on a router table against a high fence.

¼ in.

⅜ in.

⅛ in.

1⅜ in.

Rail

Rabbet cuts away the stile and glue line, revealing the rail.

Stile

¼-in. space permits door to be lifted out of the lower track and swung forward for removal.

Chamfer eases insertion and removal of door.

1⅜ in.

½ in.

1½ in.

Rail

Door rides on this ridge, not on the bottom of the groove.

Rabbet, ⅛ in. by ⅛ in.

13¾ in.

Panels are Port Orford cedar, ¼ in. thick.

15¾ in.

18⅝ in.

DRAWER BOX

The solid wood box is a separate component, which is indexed on a pin, and can be removed if necessary. Inset sides facilitate fitting and create clearance on both sides of an opened drawer.

Top, bottom, and side panels, ⅝ in. thick

¾ in.

Drawer dividers, ⁹⁄₁₆ in. thick

Stopped groove mates with spline in the side of the box.

⅜-in. setback

14⅛ in.

All drawers are 14⅛ x 11½ x 2½.

9⅞ in.

12½ in.

17¾ in.

Sliding Doors Left Open

I like sliding cabinet doors. They suit my Japanese-inspired aesthetic, and they are basic to make and quick to fit. They work equally well as flat, unframed, veneered panels (even decorated with marquetry or inlay work) or, as in this case, traditional frame-and-panel constructions of solid wood. They do have limitations, both aesthetic and functional. Foremost among these are the (aesthetic) fact that two doors need to lie in separate planes and the (functional) fact that, unless the doors are completely removed from the cabinet, only one side of it can be open at a time.

In this sideboard, these limitations worked to my advantage. Because I was thinking of it in part as a display case, I had originally thought to have only one upper and one lower door, with a single track in each box, so that two of the four compartments would always be open. In the end I decided on four doors because it gives more versatility and still leaves open the option of using the sideboard for display and letting one door hide behind the other.

A technical point on sliding doors: I always construct them so that the tongue at the bottom of the door does not ride on the bottom surface of the lower groove. Rather, the shoulder in front of the tongue rides on the ledge just in front of the groove. This provides for very smooth running and prevents the door from jumping out of its track. It also prevents problems that might be caused when particles of grit accumulate in the groove.

The Drawer Box: A Separate Construction

Rather than building drawer pockets directly into the cases, I decided to fit the drawers into a separate structure that would sit inside the upper right compartment. I liked the idea of this aesthetically, and it would simplify the construction as well, breaking it into discrete subassemblies as I like to do.

The construction of the drawer box is similar to that of the two larger cases—a basic, solid wood box doweled together.

But the drawer box's sides are U-shaped in plan. This permitted the box to be trimmed more easily to fit into the compartment and provided clearance on both sides of the drawers, so there is less risk of the drawers being opened into the back side of a not quite fully opened door.

The drawer box has two solid wood, horizontal dividers in it to create three drawer pockets. To hang the dividers I glued splines in stopped grooves in the box sides and cut mating grooves, stopped at the front, in the ends of the dividers.

When I was fitting the dividers, I first cut them so that they fit tightly between the box sides. Then I took the dividers to the jointer and, standing the pieces on the end grain, I took a fine pass off each end—all but the front 2 in. With the dividers trimmed this way, I could slide them home in the box easily with a little glue in the groove and have them snug up at the front nicely.

Last Bit

Among the last things to do was to install the two adjustable shelves. I fitted the shelves to their compartments and made brass pins to hang them on. I cut half-round notches in the underside of each shelf to fit the pins. This little touch gives me a nice feeling: to drop a shelf on its pins and feel it secure itself snugly in place. This somehow let me finally stand back and admire the completed sideboard.

Seth Janofsky doesn't argue the effectiveness of the dovetail joint, but for a change of pace he sometimes substitutes a handsome, half-blind, multiple through-tenon joint of his own devising.

START WITH A SQUARE GROOVE. The joint begins with blade-width grooves cut in the drawer sides. Blade height is set to half the thickness of the side. A flat-topped rip blade creates a clean, square-topped kerf.

MINIMORTISES. Using a horizontal mortiser and a ⅛-in.-dia. end mill bit, the author cuts through-mortises in the drawer sides exactly aligned with the table-sawn groove.

QUICK SAW. A thin saw makes quick work of cutting the tenons.

CHISEL OUT THE MIDDLE. Between the tenons where the handsaw won't reach, the author chops out the waste with a bench chisel. The waste can also be removed with the part held upright on a table saw crosscut sled.

LONG TONGUE. In the first step toward making tenons, a tongue is made at each end of the drawer fronts and backs with two cuts on the table saw. The tongue is as long as the sides are thick.

FILE IT AWAY. A file is used to square up the round corners left by the mortiser. This takes time, so be sure to use a sharp file small enough to maneuver easily.

MARK THROUGH THE MORTISES. To mark out the tenons, the author pushes the tongues into the grooves. Then he traces the mortises with a sharp pencil.

GOING HOME. The completed drawer, ready to be glued up and then veneered front and back.

A NEW FACE. Thick, shop-sawn veneers are glued to the front and back, tidying up and strengthening the joint.

APT JOINERY. Squared-off tenons suit the author's largely rectilinear sideboard.

GARY ROGOWSKI

Build a Harvest Table

I invited the entire family over for Thanksgiving dinner last year. Parents, siblings, spousal units, kidlings, and significant others—all were welcome. Unfortunately, I had no table that was large enough to seat everyone. A small detail in the greater scheme of things, but an important one nonetheless if we were all to sit together as we dined.

I set out to design and build a table that was handsome, sturdy, and serviceable. And the table would have to take only a couple of days to make. I wanted it to have a clean and simple look, so I decided on

tapered legs and a painted base, with a clear finish for just the top. I also decided on loose-tenon joinery to help simplify the construction.

Because time was of the essence, I decided to try a new approach to preparing the piece for a finish. For years, I've sweated over successively finer sanding grits of sandpaper as I ground down acres of wooden surfaces. This table was going to be different. There was to be no sanding of any sort on this piece—just handplaned surfaces and edges. "Why not?" I thought. "That's how it used to be done."

SIMPLE LINES AND A NEUTRAL, PAINTED FINISH ON THE BASE MAKE THIS TABLE VERSATILE. Though built as a dining table, it also could be used as a side table or as an extra worktable in an office, den, or child's room.

So I needed a wood that planed nicely without too much effort. Fancy figure or nice color wasn't really important because the base would be painted. I checked with my local hardwood dealer and found he had 12/4 poplar in stock. That clinched it. I didn't want to spend time laminating the leg blanks from thinner boards, so poplar it would be.

TAPERING THE LEGS

I tapered both outside faces of the table legs from their tops down to the floor. To get a taper I liked, I experimented with patterns made of hardboard until I was satisfied. I ended up with a leg that tapered from 2½ in. at the top to 1 in. at the floor.

To cut these tapers, I used my table saw and a taper jig I built specifically for these legs (see the sidebar on p. 42). The jig took only about 10 to 15 minutes to build and ensured consistent tapers.

I cut the first taper and then rotated the leg so that the cut face was face up in the jig, and so the leg would fit snugly in the jig for the second cut. I then made the second taper cut. I cleaned up the sawmarks by passing the legs over the jointer, which was set for a light cut—less than ¹⁄₁₆ in.

MORTISING LEGS AND RAILS

After tapering the legs, I routed the mortises for the loose tenons, which are separate pieces of tenon stock that are inserted into a pair of mortises (in the leg and rail, in this case). The beauty of using loose tenons is the speed with which you can join a piece of furniture.

For all the loose-tenon mortises, I used a plunge router outfitted with a ¾-in. template guide, a ½-in. up-spiral bit, and a basic shop-built fixture. The fixture consists of a piece of hardboard with a slot for a router template guide, screwed to a squared piece of hardwood that serves as a fence. I used the wedge-shaped offcuts from the tapering operation for pads on the legs to prevent them from being marred by the clamp heads and to simplify clamping the fixture to the legs.

I used the fixture for both the legs and the rails. But because these pieces are of

(see the sidebar on p. 42)

◼ Loose Tenon Joinery

SIMPLE ROUTER MORTISING FIXTURE WORKS FOR LEG AND RAIL. A slotted piece of hardboard screwed to a hardwood block provides all the guidance you'll need for routing accurate mortises. A spacer inserted between fence and rail correctly positions the template for the rail mortises.

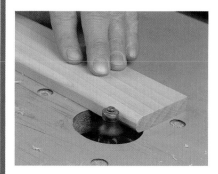

A ¼-IN. ROUNDOVER BIT PUTS A GOOD EDGE ON ½-IN. TENON STOCK. Experiment on scrap to get the bit height right, and keep the tenon stock long until you round it over.

A COUPLE OF PASSES WITH A HANDPLANE TAKE THE TENON STOCK DOWN TO SIZE. The author mills the tenon stock a hair thick, so he can get a precise fit for each joint with a plane.

different thicknesses, I built the fixture to accommodate the wide legs. Then I used a spacer to reposition the slot in the fixture when I routed the rail mortises (see the top photo on p. 39). I clamped the rails in my vise and marked their ends. Then I put the spacer between fixture and rail, positioned the fixture, clamped the whole assembly, and mortised the rail.

For a little flair, I added a detail in the bottom edge of each of the rails. I drilled a 1¼-in. hole into the rails at the bottom edge, creating something a bit fuller than a half-circle (see the photo on p. 38). I bored these holes with a Forstner bit on my drill press.

PREPARING FOR A FINISH WITH A HANDPLANE

I like to prepare all surfaces for finishing before glue-up. This usually means sanding for days on end (or at least it seems that way), going through sheets of sandpaper, and a dust mask or two. For this project, though, I had decided that any smoothing I was going to do would be with a hand-plane. So I sharpened the blade on my smoothing plane, adjusted it for a tissue-thin shaving, and planed all the legs and rails in a matter of hours. The swoosh of the blade against wood was the only sound in the shop. Then I beveled all the corners of the pieces with my block plane and turned to making tenon stock.

MAKING AND FITTING TENON STOCK

I stuck with poplar for the loose tenons, but you could use almost any scrap you have lying around. It's a good idea to mill up some extra stock, just in case. Besides, once you're set up, the process goes very quickly.

I milled the tenon stock a hair thicker than my mortise, leaving the stock fairly long (each piece about a foot), so I could rout the edges of the stock with a round-over bit on my router table (see the center photo on p. 39). A ¼-in. radius bit set to the right height will give your tenon stock an edge that will match the rounded corners of a ½-in. mortise nicely. Experiment on scrap planed to the same thickness until you get it right. Once I'd rounded the tenon stock, I cut it to length in a crosscut box on my table saw.

I used a handplane to fit the loose tenons to their respective mortises. Setting them in a bench hook, I took a shaving or two off each until they fit snugly into their mortises (see the bottom photo on 39). The tenons shouldn't be so tight that you have to hammer them into the mortises, but you shouldn't be able to pull them out of the mortises easily either.

GLUING UP IN SECTIONS

I glued up this table in sections (see the top photo on the facing page): the loose tenons into all the rails, the long rails into the legs and, finally, the two long-rail assemblies connected with the short rails. This method made gluing and clamping relatively easy. Trying to glue up the whole table at once is much more hectic.

I glued the loose tenons into the rails and then drilled ¼-in. holes about ¾ in. from the ends of the rails on the inside, pegging the tenons with sections of dowel. I dry-fitted the long-rail assembly to make sure the tenons weren't too long, and I checked the legs to see that they remained square to the rail when I clamped the joints. Then I glued the long rails into the legs. I clamped the assembly together and checked the legs again to make sure they hadn't twisted under clamping pressure.

After giving the glue time to dry (four hours or so), I planed the tops of the rails flush with the tops of the legs. It's pretty simple to put the long-rail assemblies in a vise and then plane the rails flush. Waiting until the base is completely assembled makes it a little tougher.

Before I glued the two long-rail assemblies together, I dry-fitted the joints so there would be no surprises. Then I put

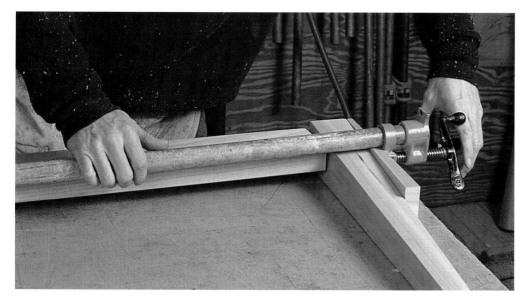

GLUING AND CLAMPING UP ONE ASSEMBLY AT A TIME MAKES THE JOB A LOT LESS HARRIED. After gluing the tenons into the long rails, the author glues and clamps the rail and two legs together to make one side of the table. Offcuts from the tapering operation make good clamping blocks.

some glue in the mortises and a little on the tenons and pulled the rails home, making sure the shoulders of the rails fit snugly against the legs (see the photo at right). I measured the diagonals of the table to see whether it had clamped up square. It was within $\frac{1}{16}$ in., so I didn't have to clamp across the table diagonally.

Once the joints were dry, I planed the tops of the short rails flush with the tops of the legs and made sure the table sat flat on the floor. I decided to use metal tabletop fasteners to secure the top to the base, so I used a biscuit joiner to cut small recesses in the rails about $\frac{1}{2}$ in. down from the top edge.

FINISHING THE BASE AND PEGGING THE TENONS

The clock was still ticking away, so I needed a quick finish for this piece. I decided on milk paint for the base. This centuries-old finish dries quickly, is easy to apply (and clean up after), and, with a clear coat over it, resists water spotting. It's very durable.

Because I had handplaned all surfaces, I didn't need to wet-sand before painting. Planed surfaces aren't abraded, so even a water-based finish like milk paint doesn't raise the grain appreciably. I put on two coats of milk paint, lightly sanding—

TWO SHORT RAILS CONNECT THE LONG-RAIL ASSEMBLIES TO COMPLETE THE BASE. Adjust the clamping pressure above and below the tenon locations to keep the shoulders tight against the legs.

I make my living as a woodworker, so I need to spend more time making furniture than making jigs or fixtures. My approach to jig making is no-nonsense: What's going to give me accurate, consistent results, safely and quickly? Which brings me to my taper jig.

This is a dedicated jig (that is, it's for one taper only; it's not adjustable), so it isn't as versatile as it might be. But it more than makes up for that in safety. The leg is captured front and back rather than just in the back, as is the case with most adjustable jigs. I've made three more harvest tables since the first one, and I've been able to depend on this jig for consistent tapers.

To make the jig, I ripped a piece of plywood about 6 in. wide (the width isn't important, but this feels about right to me) and about 3 in. longer than the leg I'm tapering. At the back edge of this plywood, I screwed a fairly wide block of wood, so I'd have a sturdy back stop. I made sure this block was flush with the bottom edge of the plywood and was sticking out far enough from the edge of the plywood to act as a stop for the leg (see the drawing below). The top of the leg will fit against this stop.

The leg bottom is the first part to enter the sawblade. It needs to be set out away from the plywood base of the jig a distance equal to the amount you want to remove. For this table, I wanted to taper the legs from 2½ in. at the top

down to 1 in. at the bottom, so i needed to push the leg bottom out 1½ in. from the edge of the plywood.

To do this, I made another stop that positively located the leg 1½ in. from the edge of the plywood. I cut two rabbets in this stop at 90° to each other, one indexing against the plywood and the other securing the bottom of the leg. I screwed this stop onto the plywood.

If the leg doesn't fit snugly between these stops, glue on a piece of sandpaper or some other shim to make sure it does. When you run those legs through the blade, with over 2½ in. of blade protruding from the table, you want to know the leg is positively captured in the jig, not vibrating around.

■ Basic Taper Jig

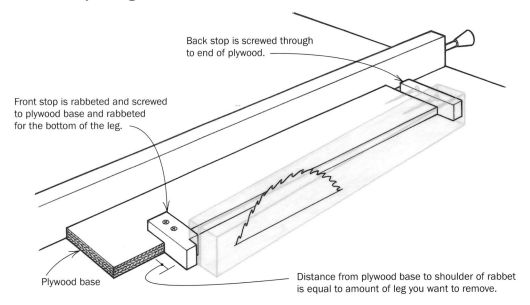

Back stop is screwed through to end of plywood.

Front stop is rabbeted and screwed to plywood base and rabbeted for the bottom of the leg.

Plywood base

Distance from plywood base to shoulder of rabbet is equal to amount of leg you want to remove.

DEDICATED TAPER JIG ENSURES SAFE, CONSISTENT RESULTS. With stops both front and back, this jig captures the leg snugly, keeping it from vibrating or moving as it's cut.

AFTER THE FIRST TAPER CUT, turn the leg so the cut faces up. This keeps a jointed face on the saw table and a square end against each stop for the second cut.

I mean, rubbing each down—after they'd dried (okay, so I sanded, but with 400-grit and only for a couple of minutes). After waiting overnight for the second coat to dry thoroughly, I gave the base a coat of Danish oil. This tends to darken milk paint significantly, so make up a sample piece first to see if you like the color change.

I wanted to peg the loose-tenon joints in the legs with a pin that contrasted with the paint, so I used a natural birch dowel against the black paint. I made up a drilling guide to use with a hand-held drill. This guide is simply a piece of hardwood scrap with a ¼-in. hole in it at the proper distance from an edge. Setting the guide against the leg put the hole right where I needed it. I cut dowels to length, drove them nearly home (I left them slightly proud) and chamfered their ends.

Making, Finishing, and Attaching the Top

I made the tabletop of poplar as well, saving the best boards for where they would be seen and appreciated. I beveled the edges of the top on the table saw and then hand-planed the top, taking care to plane in the right direction so that I didn't get any tearout. I also eased all the sharp edges on the top with a block plane.

I wanted a durable, clear finish for the top, so I brushed on three coats of a water-based polyurethane, waiting two to three hours between coats, as the manufacturer recommends.

The harvest table was completed with hours to spare. Of course, I had to borrow a few chairs, but another holiday, I'll come up with another quick project for that.

DETAILS MAKE THE DIFFERENCE. Circular cutouts in the rail centers and contrasting dowels are simple touches that add visual interest.

DAVID TUTTLE

Knockdown Computer Desk

OUTFITTED FOR THE INFOR-MATION AGE, this computer desk breaks down for transport or storage, has a power switch, and is wired for a monitor, printer, phone, and fax. Roll-out trays allow access to the keyboard and to the central processing unit (CPU).

When I bought my computer, I knew that I'd have to build a desk for it because the computer's main component, the central processing unit (CPU), was housed vertically in a tower case that wouldn't fit on my old desk. Besides that, the old desk took up too much space, and it couldn't be broken down easily for trans-

port or storage. Furthermore, it had no place for wiring, and I didn't want to look at a bunch of tangled cords and cables.

So I designed a computer desk with a top work surface, a side cabinet for an upright CPU, a pullout tray for a keyboard and mouse, and an upper shelf for a monitor. Because my wife and I would be using the desk for both office work and studying, I included wiring provisions for a printer, modem, and phone/fax. I also added a lower shelf to hold books and software, and I made a foldout extension for spreading out documents and for using a joystick (see detail B on p. 46). To reduce costs, I built the desk using edge-banded plywood—also good for its strength and durability. And to make the desk knockdown, I made threaded inserts to fasten the parts together (see the sidebar on p. 49).

Since I made my first desk, I've built three others, each time making improvements. Before I tell you how I built the latest desk, I'll talk about the requirements for a computer's CPU.

CPU CABINET

The core of my computer desk is the side cabinet for the CPU. I installed a bottom tray on drawer slides, so I can pull out the CPU to get to the wires in back. I also mounted a small drawer in the top of the case. The cabinet will house a tower case or a standard PC unit standing on edge (check

Computer Desk Assembly

The heart of the computer desk is the CPU cabinet (see detail A on p. 46). The desk, which has a sliding keyboard tray and foldout extension (see detail B on p. 46), knocks down into our other subassemblies: left side of desk, desktop with upper shelf, lower shelf with cable chase, and CPU cabinet.

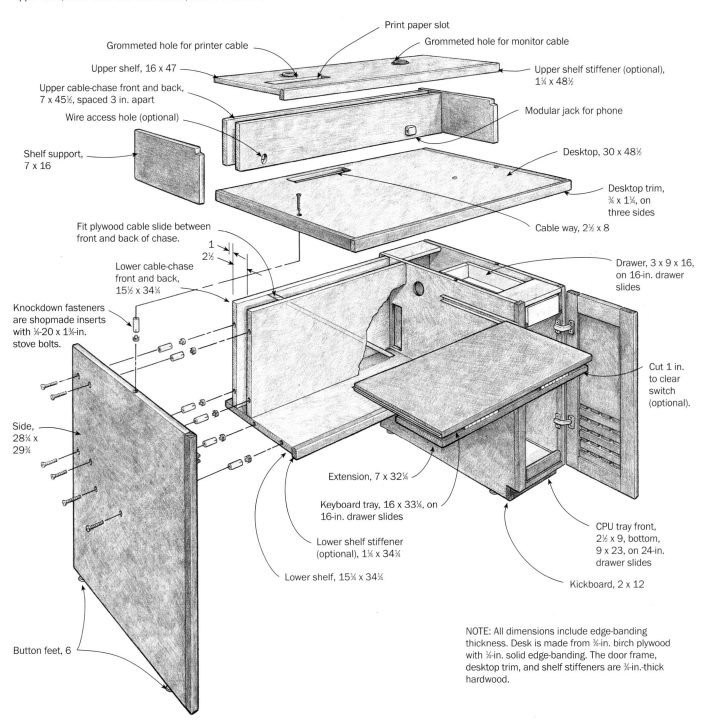

Print paper slot

Grommeted hole for printer cable

Grommeted hole for monitor cable

Upper shelf, 16 x 47

Upper shelf stiffener (optional), 1¼ x 48½

Upper cable-chase front and back, 7 x 45½, spaced 3 in. apart

Wire access hole (optional)

Modular jack for phone

Shelf support, 7 x 16

Desktop, 30 x 48½

Desktop trim, ¾ x 1¼, on three sides

Fit plywood cable slide between front and back of chase.

Cable way, 2½ x 8

Drawer, 3 x 9 x 16, on 16-in. drawer slides

Lower cable-chase front and back, 15½ x 34¼

Knockdown fasteners are shopmade inserts with ¼-20 x 1¾-in. stove bolts.

Side, 28¼ x 29¾

Cut 1 in. to clear switch (optional).

Extension, 7 x 32¼

Keyboard tray, 16 x 33¼, on 16-in. drawer slides

CPU tray front, 2½ x 9, bottom, 9 x 23, on 24-in. drawer slides

Lower shelf stiffener (optional), 1¼ x 34¼

Lower shelf, 15¼ x 34¼

Kickboard, 2 x 12

Button feet, 6

NOTE: All dimensions include edge-banding thickness. Desk is made from ¾-in. birch plywood with ¼-in. solid edge-banding. The door frame, desktop trim, and shelf stiffeners are ¾-in.-thick hardwood.

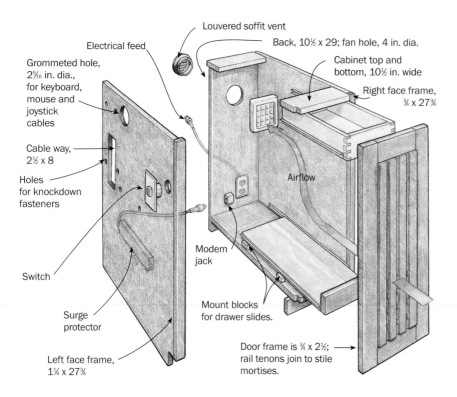

Louvered soffit vent

Electrical feed

Back, 10½ x 29; fan hole, 4 in. dia.

Grommeted hole, 2⁵⁄₁₆ in. dia., for keyboard, mouse and joystick cables

Cabinet top and bottom, 10½ in. wide

Right face frame, ¾ x 27¾

Cable way, 2½ x 8

Airflow

Holes for knockdown fasteners

Switch

Modem jack

Surge protector

Mount blocks for drawer slides.

Left face frame, 1¼ x 27¾

Door frame is ¾ x 2½; rail tenons join to stile mortises.

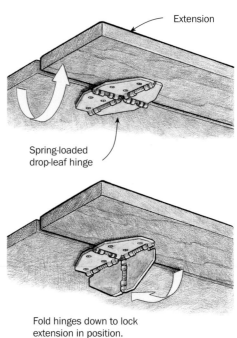

Extension

Spring-loaded drop-leaf hinge

Fold hinges down to lock extension in position.

your manual to see if this is safe for your unit). Drawing detail A (above) shows the setup that will accommodate most units. However, for large tower CPUs, you may have to eliminate the top drawer.

Component cooling and computer hardware

The CPU cabinet has a muffin fan at the rear for exhaust air, and a grid of intake holes in the front door admits cool air to the CPU. To cover the fan opening, I used a 4-in.-dia. louvered soffit vent, which I bought at my building-supply store. I formed the intake holes by cutting dadoes into the door's panel (see drawing detail A).

You should purchase all the wiring and computer-related hardware ahead of time because it will determine the sizes of the openings to cut. You can pick up a fan and

the wiring accessories, such as switches and cable, at your local computer-supply store. While you're at it, buy several cable grommets and a print-paper slot (Doug Mockett & Co. Inc. PO Box 3333, Manhattan Beach, CA 90266). You'll also need a few work boxes, receptacles, and connectors (any electrical-supply store should have them) and wire-holding clips (from hardware and auto-parts stores). The final computer-related items you may need are a surge protector, a longer keyboard cable (the ones furnished with most systems are too short), and speaker cable if you have a multimedia computer.

CONSTRUCTING THE DESK

Aside from the CPU cabinet, the desk consists of a side, a top, two cable chases (places to run wires) in the back, a keyboard tray (and extension), and upper and lower shelves. You can cut out all these parts from less than two and a half 4×8 sheets of ¾-in. plywood. I chose birch-veneer plywood because it looks nice either stained or finished natural and costs one-third the price of cherry veneer plywood. Mark out the plywood parts in light pencil, cut them out, and stack them in their subassemblies and in order.

Next rip out 40 lin. ft. of ⁵⁄₁₆-in.-thick edge-banding from straight-grained cherry or birch. Joint the strips to ¹³⁄₁₆ in. wide. Then plane the rough side of the strips to ¼ in. wide. Also, prepare stock for the drawer, door stile and rails, face frame, kickboard, top edges, and for shelf stiffeners.

Edge-banding and solid trim

Cut the banding pieces about 4 in. longer than the part you're edging. Spread glue down one edge of the plywood, and begin tacking about 3 in. from one end. Make sure the strips are proud of the plywood on both sides. Usually I tack the strips with my pneumatic nail gun (see the photo above), placing brads every 6 in. or so. If I hammer them, I'll go back to set the brad heads. Later, I fill over the heads.

Using biscuits and glue (see the photo at right), attach the desktop's solid trim, the shelf stiffeners, and the front face frames of the desk and CPU case. Clamp up each subassembly, and leave them to dry overnight. The next day, trim all the edge-banding and solid strips to length. I use an offset dovetail saw for this, following the plywood edge as a guide. Next trim all the banding to width, using a ½-in. flush-trimming bit and router jig.

Routing openings and installing inserts

You could cut all the round holes for cable passes, fan, and switch with a sabersaw, but you'll get a cleaner hole if you use a circle-cutting router jig with a ¼-in. mortising bit, as shown in the top photo on p. 48. Be sure

GLUED AND TACKED EDGE-BANDING. To protect the desk's plywood sides, lower shelf, and keyboard tray, Tuttle edge-bands the exposed edges. After tacking a band's ends, he uses a pneumatic gun to nail along the length. Once the glue is dry, he trims the banding even with the plywood, using a router and flush-trimming jig.

A PLATE-JOINED STRIP OF HARDWOOD trims the CPU cabinet side. The biscuits strengthen the joint and keep the pieces aligned during assembly.

TUTTLE MADE A CIRCLE-CUTTING JIG to rout holes for the desk's wiring grommets and for the CPU cabinet's exhaust vent.

to round over the holes for cables if you're not using grommets. To rout out the rectangular holes, use a fence or clamp a guide parallel to the edge of the plywood.

After you've made all your threaded inserts, as described in the sidebar on the facing page, it's time to drill all their holes. Bore the ½-in.-dia. holes 1¼ in. deep, using a doweling jig (see the photo below). Next glue and tap in the dowels along one edge of each of the parts. Allow them to dry an hour before you turn them over to glue the inserts in the opposite edges.

Making the door and prefinishing parts

Prepare the door-frame parts, including mortises and tenons, but before you assemble the frame and panel, cut dadoes for the air-intake holes near where your CPU's grill will be (see detail A on p. 46). I learned this intersecting-dadoes trick from a friend, Malcolm Ford. You can cut the dadoes either with a router or a table saw, but be sure to plow out only half the thickness of the panel on each side.

Sand all the parts with 120-, 180-, and then 220-grit paper, and dust everything off. It's a good idea to stain and finish the parts while they're flat and unassembled. That way, you won't have to reach into tight corners or scrape away finish drips. Use sanding sealer and a topcoat or two of polyurethane, which offers the best protection against scratches and spilled coffee.

Assembly and wiring

Plate-join the CPU cabinet together; then put the cable chases and top together. Add the drawer and button feet to the sides, and install the special table-leaf hinges (Lee Valley Tools, PO Box 1780, Ogdensburg, NY 13669) for the extension tray, if you want one. Then hang the door using Euro-style, self-closing hinges with rubber stoppers. Install the electrical boxes for the switched receptacles, and secure the wires with the plastic clips. Finally, cover the exposed heads of the knockdown fas-

DRILLING HOLES FOR THREADED INSERTS. With masking tape wrapped around a bit to mark the depth, the author uses a doweling jig and a cordless drill to bore holes for the knockdown fasteners. Next Tuttle will coat each hole with glue. He'll tap the inserts into the holes (T-nuts first) until the dowel ends are flush.

teners with plastic caps (also carried by Lee Valley Tools).

To ready the desk for your computer, it's wise to run the printer and monitor cables and cords first. It takes some patience to thread all of them through, but the slide-out CPU shelf makes this much easier. Be sure to leave some slack in the cables and cords, and then tuck them out of sight in the case.

SHOPMADE THREADED INSERTS

The first time I assembled the desk, I used zinc threaded inserts. But with just average wear and tear, the joints failed. This was because the inserts pulled out of the fir/spruce core of the plywood too easily. Not only that, the inserts' ¼-20 threads were coarse and unsightly, and some of the soft threads stripped off.

On the next desk I built, I still wanted the joints to be knockdown yet handle the stress. So I chose a shopmade variation of a threaded insert. I learned how to make the fasteners from a drawing table project in *Tage Frid Teaches Woodworking— Book 3: Furnituremaking* (The Taunton Press). The inserts consist of drilled out hardwood dowels, screws, and 10-24 threaded T-nuts. The 1-in.-long dowels provide enough gluing area, so the inserts aren't likely to tear out of the plywood edges.

To make your own threaded inserts (15 are needed for the desk) begin with ½-in.-dia. hardwood dowel stock. Drill a few ½-in. holes in some scrap, and then test-fit the dowel to be sure it fits snugly in your bit's holes. Cut about twenty-five 1-in.-long dowels.

Drilling dowel ends is difficult because the bit wanders off center in end grain. To solve this problem, make a holding jig for your drill press like Tage Frid's (see the photo at right). I found the jig works well at boring ¼-in. holes through short dowels. Even so, plan to lose a few dowels due to misalignment or grain defects; I wound up tossing out four or five.

Once you have approximately 20 bored dowels, take T-nuts and, one at a time, straighten their three prongs. Place one in each hole, and lightly tap them to mark the ends. Remove the nuts, and with a dovetail saw, make kerfs for the prongs. (Don't try to mass-produce inserts by sizing prongs from only one T-nut. The prongs are not all exactly the same.) As you saw, tilt the blade so that you match any remaining slope in each prong. Tap in the T-nuts to their mating dowels. Again, plan to lose a couple of dowels; even with the kerfing precautions, I ended up having a few dowels split. When you're done, you should have enough 10-24 threaded inserts for the job.

A DOWEL-DRILLING FIXTURE clamps to a drill-press table to hold dowels vertical and steady while their ends are bored for T-nuts (foreground). The fixture's arm, which has a fixed half and a hinged half, grasps a cut dowel as the spindle is lowered. Next Tuttle will slice the dowel end to accept the T-nut prongs.

JOHN BURCHETT

Building an Open-Pedestal Table

The open framework that supports the elliptical table shown in the photo on this page has a light and airy look that belies its strength. Doubled members that form the feet and tabletop rails, as shown in the drawing on the facing page, reduce overall mass, add interesting detail, and simplify joining the legs to the feet and rails.

In addition to the elementary joinery, I used some template-shaping tricks to greatly simplify construction. The elliptical top, with its gently curved edges, was shaped and edge-molded with a template-guided router. And the many duplicate parts of the base were all quickly and easily cut on a spindle shaper using a template that rides against a special fence.

THIS TABLE'S OPEN FRAME-WORK HAS AN OPEN FEEL, making it stronger than it looks. The one-piece top seats eight comfortably, and the components are easily shaped using templates.

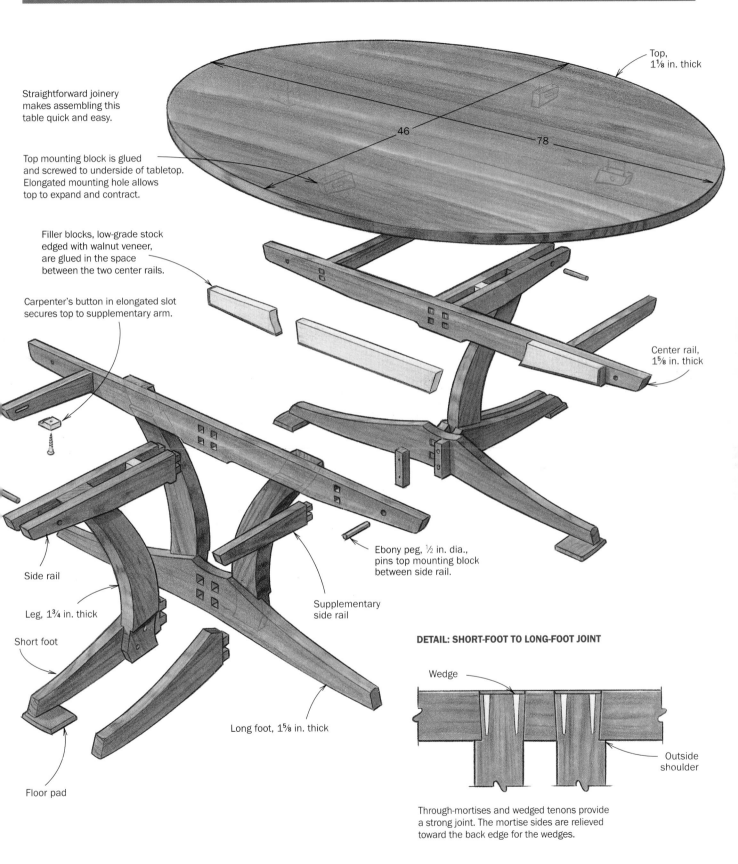

Straightforward joinery makes assembling this table quick and easy.

Top mounting block is glued and screwed to underside of tabletop. Elongated mounting hole allows top to expand and contract.

Top, 1⅛ in. thick

46

78

Filler blocks, low-grade stock edged with walnut veneer, are glued in the space between the two center rails.

Carpenter's button in elongated slot secures top to supplementary arm.

Center rail, 1⅝ in. thick

Ebony peg, ½ in. dia., pins top mounting block between side rail.

Side rail

Leg, 1¾ in. thick

Short foot

Supplementary side rail

Long foot, 1⅝ in. thick

Floor pad

DETAIL: SHORT-FOOT TO LONG-FOOT JOINT

Wedge

Outside shoulder

Through-mortises and wedged tenons provide a strong joint. The mortise sides are relieved toward the back edge for the wedges.

**DOUBLING THE FRAME MEM-
BERS REDUCES THE MASS IN
THE FEET,** legs, and tabletop
supports. It also simplifies the
joinery and adds visual interest.

WORKING WITH TEMPLATES

Templates are particularly useful for speed-
ier and more accurate small production
runs. I added extra length to the templates
for tenons and for fixing the templates to
the stock during machining. Templates that
are slightly long are safer to use because
they begin rubbing against the guide bearing or fence before the stock hits the cutter.

Any errors in the templates will be repro-
duced in every cut part, so it's worth some
extra time to be sure that the templates are
perfect.

From the full-sized front and side eleva-
tions of the table's base (see the drawing
below), I made templates for each part from
¼-in.-thick medium-density fiberboard
(MDF). I also made a quarter-arc template
of an ellipse for cutting and shaping the
top. I allowed the template to extend slightly
beyond the quarter of an ellipse limits and
outside the true circumference. That eliminates the possibility of the router cutting a
depression where one quarter meets another
when moving the template to shape the four
quarters of the top.

I've also found templates helpful for
selecting stock and laying out the cuts.
I juggled the templates around to find the
most satisfying grain configuration and eco-
nomical use of timber before cutting out
the blanks of American walnut. Then I sur-

■ Scaled Template Drawings

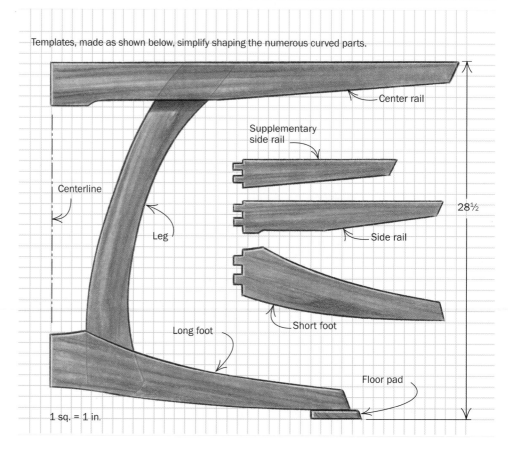

Templates, made as shown below, simplify shaping the numerous curved parts.

Center rail

Supplementary
side rail

Centerline

Leg

Side rail

28½

Long foot

Short foot

1 sq. = 1 in.

Floor pad

faced and thicknessed the blanks for shaping. I also machined the boards for the top so they could settle before remachining.

When shaping large pieces, I prefer to use a hefty, handheld router guided by a collar or bearing. But for pieces small enough to handle comfortably, I prefer a spindle shaper. The larger table, arbor, and cutters of a shaper produce a smooth, clean cut. A shaper fitted with an ordinary pair of straight-edged steel cutters and a shopmade ring fence works great for template shaping. A different fence is needed for each diameter cutter used, as shown in the photo below).

I make my ring fences from birch plywood with an arc to match the cutter's diameter and infeed and outfeed areas. The infeed and outfeed areas make shaping safer because the template can be registered against the fence, and the stock is supported before it reaches the cutter. I set the height of the ring fence with plywood spacers of varying thickness.

The templates are screwed to the blanks in areas that are cut off later. With the machine set perfectly and the waste to be removed at a minimum, the operation is safe and pleasant. After the joints were cut, I molded gentle curves on all the show edges with the shaper. I left the edges square at the leg intersections.

CUTTING THE JOINTS

Ordinarily, I cut my joints before shaping a piece so I can lay out from flat and square faces. But for this table, the base framework was bandsawn from large slabs and template-shaped to conserve timber. The only pieces that had straight reference edges were the top rails. For laying out joinery on the feet, I established a reference surface by extending a straightedge from the flat floor-contact area of the foot to the joint area. A block between the straightedge and the foot's curved section (see the photo above) kept the straightedge positioned while I marked the joint lines with a try square.

LAYING OUT JOINERY ON CURVED PIECES is difficult because there are no straight reference surfaces. The author adds blocks and straightedges as needed to overcome this problem.

RING FENCE MAKES SHAPING EASIER. It's easier to spindle-shape curved pieces with a shopmade ring fence that follows a template attached to the stock.

The first joints I cut were the tenons of the short feet and their mortises in the long feet, using the full-sized drawings to determine joint positions, as shown in the drawing detail on p. 51. The tenons on the short feet and side rails are wedged. I left them about 1/16 in. shy of the full thickness of the long foot and center rail to allow for any possible shrinkage in the thickness of the mortised members. The mortises were cut with a square, hollow-chisel mortiser, and I relieved the sides of the mortises at the back with a chisel to allow for the expansion of the wedges.

To mark the tenons at the bottom of the four legs, I clamped each leg between its corresponding feet and scribed the curved shoulder line on each side of each leg. I hogged off the tenon waste on the radial-arm saw and cleaned up the tenon surface with a shoulder plane. The convex curves of the shoulders were pared with a chisel.

I dry-assembled and clamped the legs and feet to mark the tenons at the upper ends of the legs. The shoulders were scribed and the tenons cut as before. At this stage, I marked and cut one joint at a time and assembled and clamped it together while I

marked the next joint. Assembling a project one step at a time seems the only way to proceed in custom work involving curved shapes. In fact, this is the way I approach most of my cabinet work. Still, I've found it necessary to make small adjustments to the top joints at final assembly after the bottom joints were glued.

THE ASSEMBLY PROCEDURE

To simplify assembly, I glued up the base into two units, each consisting of a long foot, a pair of short feet, and a leg.

Clamping shaped work calls for some ingenuity, but I find it is this sort of challenge that makes woodworking interesting. I overcame the problem of clamping the short feet to the long foot by adding blocks to the outside faces of the short feet, as shown in the photo below. These blocks provide a bearing surface for clamps to pull the joint together. A softwood block between the pair of short feet holds the feet at the correct spacing. I glued abrasive to the blocks on the outside of the feet to prevent slipping when the joint is clamped. I checked this assembly dry and pulled the

CLAMPING LONG AND ODD-SHAPED PIECES. Blocks are clamped to the sides of the short feet with a properly sized spacer between each pair of feet. The blocks provide surfaces parallel to the long foot to apply clamping pressure during glue-up.

joint apart with the short feet still clamped together with their spacing block. Then I glued the mortises and reinserted the tenons. The two main clamps were tightened, everything checked for alignment, and the wedges driven home. I cut the wedges flush with the ends of the tenons. The same clamping arrangement was used to glue the side rails and the supplementary side rails into the long rails.

I checked the accuracy of the shoulder lines of the legs to the feet and made fine adjustments to the tops of the feet, using a scraper rather than trying to alter the shoulders themselves. To clamp the leg in place during glue-up, I screwed through a block spanning the bottom of the feet and into the end of the leg to pull the shoulder tight to the top of the foot.

The upper part of the frame was fairly straightforward; it glues into two half-assemblies consisting of one center rail, a pair of side rails, and two supplementary rails. One of the half-assemblies was glued and clamped in place to three of the legs. Filler pieces, their lower edges already veneered with walnut, were then glued and screwed in place, as shown in the drawing on p. 51, to form tight-fitting mortises at the tops of the legs. The second half-assembly was then glued in place.

Apart from making the four floor pads, the only remaining work on the frame was shaping and drilling the four walnut blocks that attach the top. These blocks, which fit between the ends of the paired rails, are screwed, counterbored, and plugged on the underside of the tabletop. The blocks are held to the rails with ½-in.-dia. ebony pegs. The holes in the blocks between the short rails are elongated to allow the top to expand and contract.

GLUING UP THE TOP

I handplaned the edges for the simple butt joints I used to glue up the top. Two details are worth mentioning when handplaning or shooting a joint: controlling the plane and checking for square.

To control the cut, the left hand does not hold the plane's foreknob but grips the plane's side near the front with thumb on top and index finger rubbing against the side of the wood being jointed. The rubbing finger provides the control needed to move the plane either left or right to adjust the squareness of the cut.

When checking for squareness, the square should be held with its body on the planed edge and the blade extended down the face of the timber. The angle between the long blade and the face exaggerates error, making inaccuracies obvious.

I glued up the top with the heartwood facing up to avoid any exposed sapwood on the tabletop. That way, any cupping would be convex on the upper surface and easier to restrain than a concave top.

After edge-gluing the timbers, I cut the completed slab to a rough elliptical shape and handplaned it flat, planing first across the grain and then along the grain. I cut the slab to a true ellipse with a straight, two-flute router bit, using the ellipse template and a collar-guided router. I couldn't find a stock router bit to cut the gentle curve I wanted on the top's edge, and I didn't want to wrestle the heavy top across the spindle shaper. So I reground a straight router bit and worked the lower part of the curve first with the top upside down. Then I reground the cutter to a slightly more pronounced curve before turning the top over to work the upper part of the curve. I finished off this asymmetrical scotia shape by fairing the two cuts together with a curved scraper, constantly referring to a template to keep the edge uniform.

FINISHING UP

I gave the underframe a couple of coats of linseed oil and polished it off with three coats of dark wax. Because the top receives more abuse, I applied several coats of a mix of linseed oil, polyurethane, and mineral spirits as a base for 14 coats of hand-rubbed, hot, raw linseed oil applied over a month. The client continued the finishing process by applying a coat each month for the next 12 months.

DAVID FAY

Frame-and-Panel Bed

A BED MADE IN THREE TYPES OF WOOD. The framework, including the posts, is made of cherry. The panels are resawn, slip-matched pear wood. Accent strips along the inside of the frames and along the bottoms of the bed rails are granadillo.

M y favorite designs have come to me unexpectedly, in a flash of an idea, far away from the drafting table. The ensuing challenge to develop that vision into a finished product requires a lot of time spent refining what may seem like small details.

I begin with a sketch, nothing fancy or beautiful. The back of an envelope or napkin will do. Drawing this way frees me from the constraints of trying to perfect the piece; all I'm after is getting the inspiration down on paper.

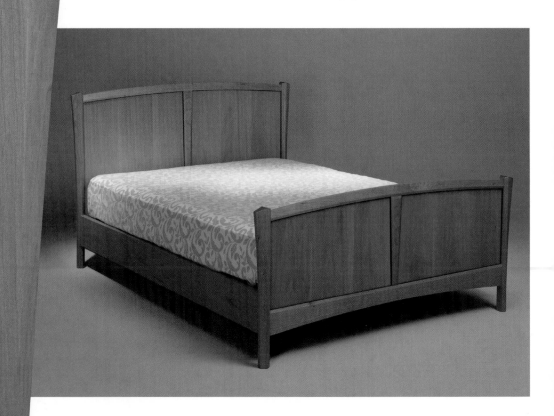

If the piece is a commission, the next step is listening to the customer. That often influences the dimensions of a project. For this bed, the customer wanted a queen-sized frame that could accommodate a futon mattress or a standard box-spring and mattress set. As a result, I had to make the bed rails wide enough to accommodate an adjustable inner rail.

A dimensioned drawing comes next. Although an accurate drawing can help me visualize a piece, this two-dimensional tool has limitations. That's why I build a full-scale model of any tricky parts to work out design and construction needs and to perfect technical skills.

The model allows me to evaluate how the details relate to the rest of the design. For example, I used a model to determine the proportions of the posts and rails. I experimented with the reveal at various widths. A ⅞-in. reveal looked chunky, and a ⅝-in. reveal looked skinny. But when I tried a ¾-in. reveal, it looked right. I also used the model to determine the size of the granadillo reveal as it related to the panel and posts and rails. Using the model, I was able to refine subtle details and their proportions. There's nothing scientific here, no golden rules. It's a matter of trial and error and trusting your instincts.

CUT THE JOINERY, THEN BEGIN SHAPING

The bedposts are thick at the top and get skinnier near the floor. As the thickness changes, the widths of the two faces also change. But one thing stays constant: the width of the outside edge or reveal.

All of the joints that involve the bedposts are machined while the stock is still square. These joints include the tenons for the upper and lower rails of the headboard/footboard, the mortises in the bedposts, the tenons on the long rails (see the sidebar on p. 63 to learn how to make the hidden post-to-lower-rail joints, and the grooves for the panels.

Next, lay out each post's six-sided profile on the end grain (see the top left photo in the sidebar at right). Then connect the lines

■ Shaping the Bedposts

LAY OUT THE BEDPOSTS. The six-sided shape is drawn on the end grain first, then the lines are carried over onto the faces.

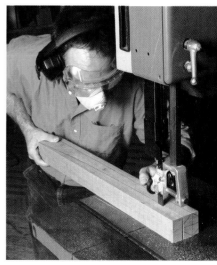

CUT THE OUTSIDE CURVE FIRST. Bandsaw close to the line.

ATTACH THE TEMPLATE TO THE POST. Clean up using a router and pattern-cutting bit.

SHAPE THE FACETS WITH AN ANGLE GRINDER. A 24-grit sanding disc removes material quickly. Use long, fluid motions and take light passes.

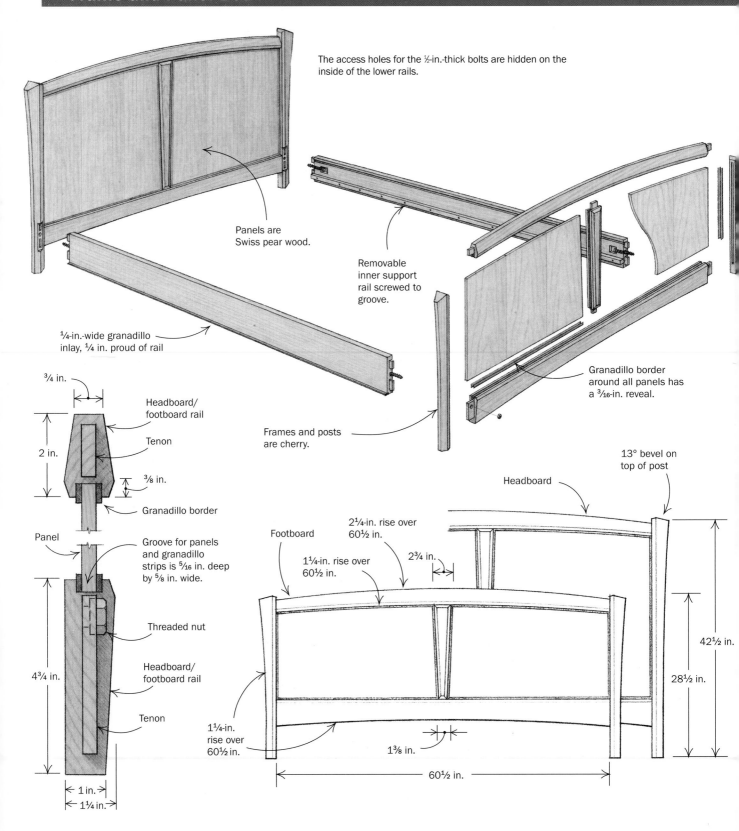

The access holes for the ½-in.-thick bolts are hidden on the inside of the lower rails.

Panels are Swiss pear wood.

Removable inner support rail screwed to groove.

¼-in.-wide granadillo inlay, ¼ in. proud of rail

Granadillo border around all panels has a ³⁄₁₆-in. reveal.

Frames and posts are cherry.

¾ in.

Headboard/ footboard rail

Tenon

2 in.

³⁄₈ in.

Granadillo border

Panel

Groove for panels and granadillo strips is ⁵⁄₁₆ in. deep by ⁵⁄₈ in. wide.

Threaded nut

Headboard/ footboard rail

4¾ in.

Tenon

1 in.

1¼ in.

13° bevel on top of post

Headboard

Footboard

2¼-in. rise over 60½ in.

1¼-in. rise over 60½ in.

2¾ in.

42½ in.

28½ in.

1¼-in. rise over 60½ in.

1³⁄₈ in.

60½ in.

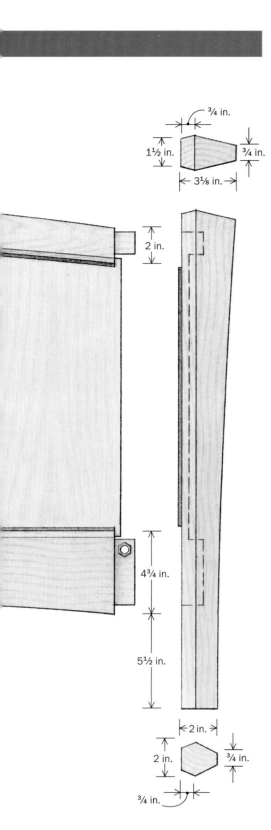

from end to end along the outside of the post—use a black, thin-line pen, which is easier to see than a pencil line.

The posts have three straight, flat sides (inside edge and the two adjoining sides), two curvy sides (on each side of the outside edge) where the plane twists, and a curved, tapered side (the outside edge with the ¾-in. reveal). Whenever possible, I make templates to lay out and cut curved parts (see the sidebar on p. 60). I use the templates to trace layout marks, and then, after bandsawing parts to rough dimensions, I attach the templates to the stock and use them with a pattern-cutting bit.

Mark the outside facet of each post using a template and bandsaw the waste (see the top right photo on p. 57). Fair the curve by attaching the same template and trimming the post with a pattern-cutting bit, as shown in the center photo on p. 57 (screw the template to the waste portions of the post). Remove the template and draw the last set of layout lines on the outside face.

Use a router with a 45Á bearing-guided bit to remove as much stock as possible from the corners of the post. Next, use an angle grinder with a 24-grit sanding disc to rough in the shape (see the bottom photo on p. 57) on the two facets of each post that curve and twist. Use long, fluid motions with this tool and don't stop in midcut. Otherwise, you end up with flat spots that break up the curve. With a light touch, you can grind smoothly and get very close to the layout lines. It takes some practice to get a feel for shaping with a grinder, and I fine-tuned my skills using scrap stock.

CLEAN UP THE POST

A No. 50 Nicholson® pattern-maker's rasp is used to fine-tune the shape. A rasp is small enough that you can follow the twist on each post.

ROUTING CURVED TEMPLATES

You don't have to figure out the radius of a curve as long as you know the rise and run. With this method, you can make perfect templates for curved work, especially wide-radius curves. Because the method involves a trapped cut, there is some danger that the router might want to find its own path, so be prepared to turn the tool off immediately if it starts getting away from you.

MAKE THE JIG

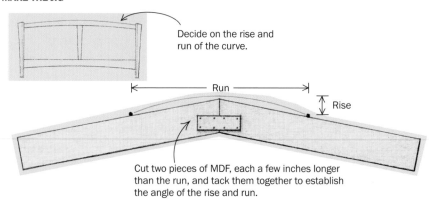

Decide on the rise and run of the curve.

Cut two pieces of MDF, each a few inches longer than the run, and tack them together to establish the angle of the rise and run.

CUT THE TEMPLATE

Place two nails or round shelf pins onto the template stock at a distance equal to the length of the template plus the diameter of the router bit.

Attach a plunge router (equipped with a ½-in. straight bit and ⅝-in. template guide) to the jig, orienting it so that the bit just touches the intersection.

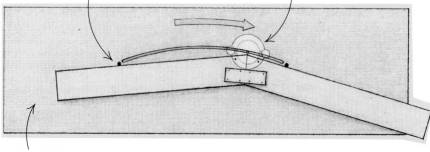

Use ½-in. MDF for the template stock. Be sure it's long enough to support both wings of the jig.

Place a large sheet of scrap below the template stock to avoid cutting the workbench.

SET THE JIG DOWN AND PUSH IT UP AGAINST THE PINS. Turn the router on, plunge in about ⅛ in., and push the jig to the right, keeping it in contact with the pins. Repeat, taking deeper cuts until you cut through the template stock. Don't let the router bit contact the pins. Finish cutting out the template on a bandsaw.

To find high and low spots left by the grinder, draw diagonal pencil lines across the faces of each post. The rasp works best cutting in short, diagonal strokes. When the deep scratches left by the 24-grit disc are gone and the curves of the posts look fair, move on to a hand scraper, paying close attention to the layout lines. Hold the post up to a light to see how it's coming along. When you run into domed sections, remove material using long, fluid motions.

Clean up further using a small sanding block. I prefer to use a small piece of medium-density fiberboard (MDF) with cork glued onto the face. It's small enough (approximately 1 in. by 1½ in.) to maneuver along the changing curves of the post. A large sanding block tends to straighten the curves instead of follow them.

Start with 180-grit sandpaper and follow up with 220 grit. If you find rasp marks on the surface, go back to the scraper, which works faster than sandpaper. Finally, use a small piece of folded 220-grit paper and hand-sand the surface with the grain. Hand-sanding is important because your fingers will sense any high or low spots. Lastly, break all of the edges with a rigid sanding block and 220-grit paper, just enough to make the edges inviting to touch yet still crisp to the eye.

Cut the top of each post on the chopsaw, then sand it smooth with a rigid (not cork) sanding block, which will bring out the figure of the end grain.

HEADBOARD AND FOOTBOARD ALSO HAVE SIX-SIDED PARTS

The upper and lower rails for the headboard and footboard are curved and have six sides to match the posts (see the drawings on p. 58). The procedure for building the headboard and footboard is similar to the posts. First, cut the joints while the stock is still square. (The only exceptions are the center stiles. Take their measurements off the frames of the headboard and footboard after dry-fitting them. Cut the mortises for the center stiles by hand.) Then mark the six-sided profiles on the shoulders of all of the tenons.

As you did with the posts, make a template to help lay out and cut the curves of the headboard and footboard rails. Mark the curves using the template, then roughcut the parts on the bandsaw. Finish up by attaching the template to the stock and use a pattern-cutting bit and router. Before shaping the facets of the rails, cut the slots for the accent strips and panels, using a router with a slot-cutting bit.

The same methods and tools used on the posts are used to mark, cut, and shape the rails. The center divider is cut like the rails; the tenons are cut first on the table saw. Then the tapered angles are cut; the bevels are shaped with a grinder.

Inlay Adds Contrast

DEGREE OF SEPARA-TION. Granadillo provides contrast and separation between the similarly toned cherry and pear wood.

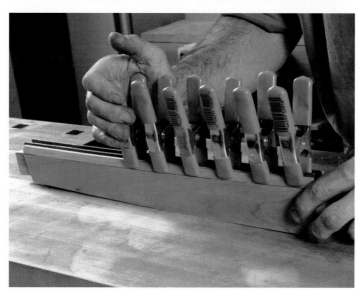

BEFORE THE JOINT IS ASSEMBLED. The granadillo strips are glued into the grooves for the panels with the help of a battery of small spring clamps.

A granadillo border separates frame from panel

The panels in this bed are made of Swiss pear wood, and the frame, posts, and rails are made of cherry. Although in time the cherry will darken more than the pear wood, the contrast in color between them, after milling, is subtle. To separate the two woods visually, the frame is inlaid with strips of granadillo, a deep, rich, purple-brown wood. The strips of granadillo surround each panel. A strip of granadillo is also inlaid along the bottom edge of the bed's rails.

Mill the granadillo strips wide and long. (Rip all of the granadillo straight; the strips will bend to conform to the curve of the rails.) Then clamp up the rails and stiles and take your measurements for the granadillo. Cut the strips to size, then glue them in place, using lots of spring clamps. Where the strips intersect, use a butt joint.

Take measurements for the panels while the headboard and footboard are clamped together. Then transfer these measurements onto ¼-in.-thick particleboard or plywood and cut these out on the bandsaw. Because of the number of curves, there's usually a bit of tweaking to get everything right. Once you have a good fit, use the ¼-in.-thick panels as templates for the real thing.

The pear-wood panels are resawn and slip-matched. Leave about ⅛ in. of extra space for every 12 in. of panel to allow for expansion and contraction of the wood. When gluing up the frame, put a dab of glue in the center of each rail's groove to keep the panel centered.

This bed frame is compatible with a futon or a box-spring and mattress set. To allow for that, cut two dadoes—one high, one low—on each long rail. For the futon, two removable inner rails are screwed to the upper grooves. (You'll also need slats to support the futon.) For use with a traditional mattress set, the inner rails are attached to the lower groove, and the box spring rests on the inner rails (see the photo on p. 64).

Decorative caps made to cover bolt holes in bedposts work fine, especially when used on traditional-looking furniture. But I didn't want a cap to detract from the fluid shape of the posts of this bed. A friend, Mike Laine, showed me how to get a strong joint by using mortise and tenons coupled with captured nuts and bolts. The joint is secure and leaves no trace of its mechanics once the bed has been assembled and a mattress or futon installed.

Refer to the drawing on p. 58 for the size and location of the joinery, which is cut while the stock is still square. Clamp and dry-fit the posts to the lower rails of the headboard and footboard, one at a time. Then, on the drill press, align a drill bit with the already drilled bolt hole in the post and drill through the tenon of the rail, being careful not to drill too deeply.

Remove the lower rail and thread the bolt through the hole and into the nut. Scribe the outline of the nut onto the tenon. The mortise for the nut captures only half its thickness; any more would weaken the tenon. To make room for the protruding half of the nut, enlarge the mortise in the bedpost around the nut with a small router and finish up with a chisel.

The bolt is housed in a dado cut into the lower rails, centered between the two tenons. Mortise around the head to give you enough clearance to reach in with a hex wrench and cinch everything down. Check the joints for fit, then epoxy the nuts in place, being careful not to get any glue on the threads.

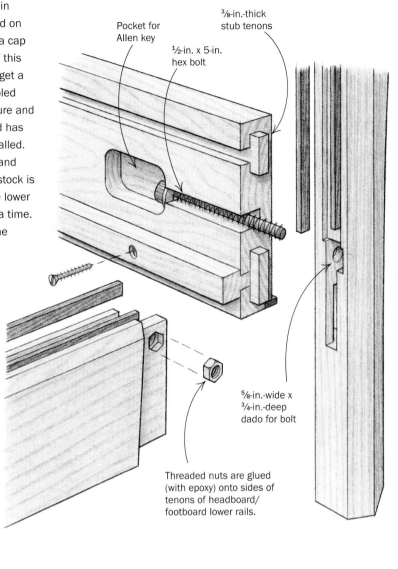

Pocket for Allen key

½-in. x 5-in. hex bolt

⅜-in.-thick stub tenons

⅝-in.-wide x ¾-in.-deep dado for bolt

Threaded nuts are glued (with epoxy) onto sides of tenons of headboard/ footboard lower rails.

FINISH WITH HAND-RUBBED OIL

I used a low-gloss tung oil to finish the bed, applying three coats over three days. When applying the first coat, the wood will be thirsty and absorb a lot of finish. Apply a liberal amount of oil to one section at a time, such as one panel. Rub off the excess after a couple of minutes and move on to another section. After a day, go over the entire piece with a green 3M® scrub pad, lightly rubbing off raised grain and built-up oil.

On the second day, apply a thin coat of oil, again working in small sections, and wipe with a clean cloth after a few minutes. For a splotch-free finish, remove the excess before it begins to dry and get gummy. On the third day, apply a final coat, the same way as the second, but use even less oil. When using oil, less is better.

MOVABLE INNER RAIL ACCOMMODATES TWO TYPES OF MATTRESSES. Placed in the lower groove, the rail is positioned for a box-spring and mattress set. In the upper slot, the rail accepts a futon (using slats for support).

CHARLES GRIVAS

Mahogany Bedside Table

THE TAPERED OCTAGONAL legs on this mahogany bedside table add an unusual element to the piece.

Legs are the cornerstones of many pieces of furniture. The tapered octagonal legs on this bedside table are a little different from the ones on some furniture in that construction and milling are integral parts of the layout of the table. Unlike most furniture construction where all the parts are milled separately and then assembled, the construction of this table involves doing some of the leg milling, then using the partially milled legs as templates for the sides and back of the piece. Also, the biscuits that hold the sides and back to the legs must be cut into the legs before all the facets of the tapered octagon are milled. Don't worry; it's not as confusing as it sounds.

The octagon at the bottom of the legs is 2 in. across, and the leg tapers to a 1½-in. octagon at the top. Laying out an octagon is simple if first you draw a square (see the drawings on p. 68). For the bottom of the leg, lay out a 2-in. square, and find its center by marking diagonal lines from the corners.

Set your compass from the corner of the square to the center. Then from the corner, swing your compass and mark a point along the two perpendicular sides that meet at that corner. Do this from all four corners of the square. You should now have two

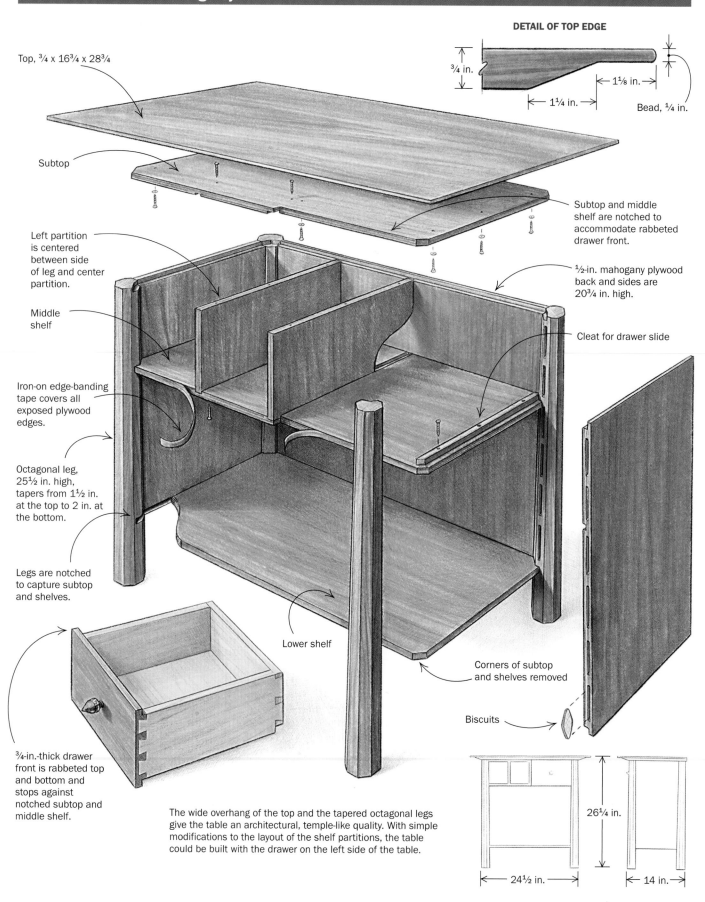

DETAIL OF TOP EDGE

3/4 in.

1 1/4 in.

1 1/8 in.

Bead, 1/4 in.

Top, 3/4 x 16 3/4 x 28 3/4

Subtop

Left partition is centered between side of leg and center partition.

Middle shelf

Iron-on edge-banding tape covers all exposed plywood edges.

Octagonal leg, 25 1/2 in. high, tapers from 1 1/2 in. at the top to 2 in. at the bottom.

Legs are notched to capture subtop and shelves.

Subtop and middle shelf are notched to accommodate rabbeted drawer front.

1/2-in. mahogany plywood back and sides are 20 3/4 in. high.

Cleat for drawer slide

Lower shelf

Corners of subtop and shelves removed

Biscuits

3/4-in.-thick drawer front is rabbeted top and bottom and stops against notched subtop and middle shelf.

The wide overhang of the top and the tapered octagonal legs give the table an architectural, temple-like quality. With simple modifications to the layout of the shelf partitions, the table could be built with the drawer on the left side of the table.

26 1/4 in.

24 1/2 in.

14 in.

marks on each of the square's four sides, or eight marks in total. Each mark represents a corner of the octagon. Connect the marks, and there you have it.

Lay out a 2-in. octagon on the end grain of each of four 25-in.-long, 2-in.-sq. billets, and lay out a 1½-in. octagon on the end grain of the opposite ends. Accuracy is important, so sharpen your pencil for this.

CUT A LITTLE, MARK A LITTLE, CUT SOME MORE

Don't think of the milling of the legs as a process of making tapered octagons. Instead, think of it in two parts: making tapered squares, then turning the tapered squares into tapered octagons. I prefer to use a table-saw jig to cut tapered square legs, but there are many good methods for leg tapering. I use a jointer to turn the tapered squares into tapered octagons, then I use a handplane to dress all eight sides.

But wait! Don't go jointer and taper-jig crazy just yet. Let's take this a taper at a time because before all the tapers are cut, a partially tapered leg is used to lay out the sides and back of the table. Cut the first taper on one side of each square leg billet. The partially tapered leg will now be used to lay out the table's sides and back, and an untapered leg face will be used as a registration guide to cut biscuits in the center of the already tapered leg face.

From the drawing on the facing page, you can see that the table's rectangular footprint is 24½ in. by 14 in. and that the plywood sides and back are 20¾ in. tall. Cut a piece of plywood 24½ in. by 20¾ in. for the back. Cut the two side pieces at 14 in. by 20¾ in. Now line up a leg billet along the 20¾-in. edge of the plywood so that the tapered side of the billet faces in and an untapered side is flush with the outside edge of the plywood. Scribe a line on the plywood along the tapered side of the bil-

MAKE A SQUARE INTO AN OCTAGON

Find square's center by drawing diagonal lines. Set compass from corner to center, distance X.

From each corner, swing distance X on perpendicular sides, making a total of eight marks.

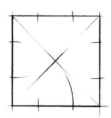

Connect eight marks to form octagon.

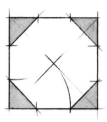

LEG ACTS AS TEMPLATE FOR PLYWOOD SIDES AND BACK. The author tapers one side of a leg and then holds an untapered, still-square edge of the leg against the square corners of the plywood and scribes along the leg's tapered edge.

GROOVED JIG CENTERS BISCUITS. To cut biscuits down the center of a tapered face of a leg, the author clamps a grooved 2×2 against the perpendicular, untapered side of the leg. The depth of the groove plus the distance from the base of the biscuit jointer to the center of its blade has to equal 1 in.—the center of the leg.

A TAPERED SQUARE BECOMES A TAPERED OCTAGON. After all four sides of the square leg are tapered, the author draws lines along the length of the legs, connecting the corners of the octagons he has drawn on the end grain. To remove the waste, he uses a jointer with the fence set at 45°.

let. Scribe similar lines along all the 20¾-in. edges of the back and sides.

CUT BISCUITS AFTER TAPERING TWO SIDES

Before you do any more leg tapering, you have to cut biscuits in the already tapered side. The table's two back legs get two perpendicular rows of six biscuits—one row to join the leg to the back of the table and one row to join a side. The front legs get a single row of six biscuits to join a leg to a side. Centering biscuits in the facets of an eight-sided tapered leg would be almost impossible. The task is easy if you cut the biscuits now while the legs have a square face to use as a guide for your biscuit jointer. A simple grooved jig cut from a 2×2, 20¾ in. long, centers the biscuits (see the center photo on the facing page).

The depth of the groove you cut in the 2×2 is determined by your brand of biscuit jointer. What's critical is that the dimension of the jig's groove plus the distance from the bottom of your biscuit jointer's base to the center of the blade equal 1 in.—the centerline of the leg billet on the untapered side. So, for instance, if the center of your biscuit jointer's blade is ⅜ in. from the bottom of the base, then the groove you cut in the jig will equal ⅝ in. Using the jig as a fence for your biscuit jointer will let you cut slots at 1 in.

After you have grooved the 2×2 jig, mark lines for six evenly spaced biscuits. Clamp the jig to the untapered leg side that is perpendicular to the one tapered side, and using the jig as a guide for your biscuit jointer, cut the slots in the tapered leg side.

For the two back legs, taper a leg side perpendicular to the side you tapered first, then cut the second row of biscuits, making sure to clamp the grooved jig to an untapered side. After all the biscuit slots are cut—two perpendicular rows in the back legs and a single row in the front legs—taper the remaining two sides of the legs.

It's time to turn the tapered squares into tapered octagons. Remember those octagons you meticulously laid out on the top and bottom of each leg billet? Your accurate layout will pay off. Use a straightedge and sharp pencil to scribe lines along the length of each square-tapered billet, connecting the corners of each end-grain octagon (see the right photo on the facing page). Once all the lines are drawn, remove the four corners of the square-tapered legs. I use a jointer with the fence set at 45 degrees, then dress the legs with a plane. Now the legs are finished, biscuit slots already cut.

DRY-FIT THE CASE, AND MARK FOR THE TOP, SHELF, AND BOTTOM

After the legs are completed, the rest is straightforward. Cut the sides and back plywood pieces along the lines you scribed with the partially tapered legs, and cut biscuits so they line up with the slots you've already cut into the legs. Cut a dado into the back and sides to accommodate the subtop, the middle shelf, and the lower shelf.

The next step is to dry-fit the case, using unglued biscuits to hold the sides and back to the legs. Rather than cut a precise notch in the plywood subtop, middle shelf, and lower shelf to go around the four octagonally faceted legs, the legs are relieved to capture the plywood. After the case is dry-fit, use a razor knife to mark the legs for the shelf locations. You could take these

DRY-FIT THE LEGS TO THE SIDES AND BACK, and then mark the legs for the subtop, the middle shelf, and the lower shelf. A square and a razor knife ensure accuracy.

NOTCH THE LEGS, NOT THE SHELVES. The subtop, middle shelf, and lower shelf are captured in the notches in the legs as well as in the dadoes in the plywood sides and back.

measurements from the dadoed back and sides, but I find that empirically marking the exact locations is more exact. It only takes a minute, and you can check for square and possibly see any mistakes or oversights that might have occurred. After marking the legs for the three horizontal shelves, disassemble the piece and notch the legs for the shelves. Cut off the four corners of the plywood pieces, so the leg notches don't have to be cut to an exact depth.

DETAILING THE TOP

The beaded and beveled edge of the table-top is somewhat reminiscent of a raised panel. I ran the edge treatment around the

■ CONSTRUCTION NOTES

The front edge of the plywood subtop and middle shelf are notched ½ in. to allow the ½-in. rabbet in the ¾-in.-thick drawer front to close flush. I used hot-glue edge-banding tape to cover the laminations on the table's exposed plywood. The tape is readily available and is applied with a clothes iron. The orange edge-trimming tool shown below is available from Constantine (800-223-8087).

The right side of the table's small drawer follows the taper of the right front leg. The taper is slight enough so that I was able to make the drawer with squared sides and then plane the edge of the drawer front to fit the leg. Trying to build a drawer with a tapered side would have been a headache, and after all the extra work involved, I'm sure I would have had to plane the drawer front anyway.

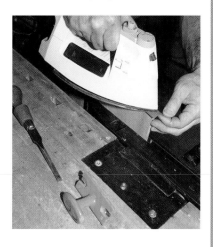

front and around both sides of the top. I left the table's back edge unadorned so that the table would fit snug to the wall next to my bed.

Molding the top is a multistep process that uses a router with a beading bit, a table saw with a dado blade, an upright cut on a table saw, and a little handwork with a rabbet plane and a smooth plane. The photos in the sidebar below explain the process.

■ Molding the Top: Milling It Is a Multistep Process

1. Begin with a ¼-in. beading bit for the top's edge treatment.

2. A dado blade set at an angle makes the second and third cuts.

3. The last cut is done with the top held upright against the table-saw fence.

4. A smooth plane and a rabbet plane dress the cuts.

MASON RAPAPORT

Curved Panels from a Vacuum Veneer Press

One of the most used tools in my shop is my vacuum veneer press. In fact, its use in creating veneered curved panels, which are the major components in all of my furniture, is absolutely fundamental. My first encounter with a vacuum press was as an apprentice to woodworker Roger Heitzman in Scotts Valley, California, in 1990. At the time, I had no idea how essential to my woodworking that tool would become.

Before the advent of vacuum presses, it was necessary, if you were laminating curved shapes, to build separate male and female forms that both mated very precisely with the layers to be laminated. The whole

VENEERED CURVES ARE EASIER WITH A VACUUM PRESS. One form and a simple caul are all that are necessary to press a curved, veneered component in a vacuum press. This table, veneered in cherry and walnut, consists of two simple laminations splinetenoned together.

assembly had to come together as a perfect sandwich, with the forms as bread and the veneers and substrate layers making up the fixings.

But with the vacuum press, I need to build only one form. The vacuum bag and cauls (layers of flexible material that distribute clamping pressure) made from whatever material I'm using as the substrate, take care of the rest. The process can be divided into four main steps: making the form, preparing the substrate and veneer, gluing up, and using the vacuum bag to clamp everything together.

MAKING THE FORM

My bending forms are pretty simple. They consist of sections of particleboard or medium-density fiberboard (MDF) that are bandsawn and routed to the exact profile of the finished curve. These sections, or ribs, are then attached to one another with spacer blocks. The result, as shown in the photo below, looks sort of like an upside down boat without its hull.

The form needs to be 2 in. or so longer than the final length of the finished lamination. This excess allows you to glue up an oversized piece that is trimmed to fit later. Don't forget to add the excess, or you'll be sorry.

Because all the ribs have to be uniform, the first step is making a master template to cut all the ribs. I start with a scale drawing of the curve I want, and then I enlarge it to full size on a sheet of ¼-in. plywood to make the template. It's important that the template be cut and sanded to a fair curve. Any dips, chips, or kinks in the edge of the template will show through on your finished piece.

BENDING FORMS ARE EASY TO MAKE. Using yellow glue and nails (or screws), you can assemble a form quickly from ribs of medium-density fiberboard (MDF). Use a combination square to make sure all the ribs are aligned.

Trace around your template onto the particleboard or the MDF, and then cut just shy of the line on a bandsaw. Next, use a router with a flush-trimming bit, following your template, to get a clean, fair curve. This process ensures that each rib will be identical.

Once the ribs are all cut, take the waste MDF and cut small pieces to use as spacers. Spacing keeps the weight of the form down but maintains sufficient rigidity so that the form will not deflect under pressure. To assemble the form, I use yellow glue, along with nails or screws, and a good combination square to make sure the form goes together square. The form should be as wide as the final piece, plus an inch or so on either side to allow for final, accurate trimming.

PREPARING SUBSTRATE

I use ⅛-in. Italian bending poplar or 1.5mm (about ¹⁄₁₆ in.) Finland birch for the substrate, depending on the radius of the curve I'm bending. The Italian poplar will bend to a radius of about 2⅛ in.; the ¹⁄₁₆-in. birch will bend to about 1 in. radius. When rough-cutting thin sheets, use an auxiliary fence or some other means to prevent the sheets from sliding under the table-saw fence. Remember to cut the sheets of plywood slightly oversize; final trimming takes place after the piece comes out of the press. Bending plywoods are available in sizes down to 0.4 mm (about ¹⁄₆₄ in.) from specialty plywood dealers, such as Harbor Sales (1000 Harbor Ct., Sudlersville, MD 21668; 800-345-1712).

PREPARING THE VENEER

If one sheet of face veneer will do the job, I just rough-cut it slightly oversize with a sharp razor knife or veneer saw. But if the face veneer has to consist of several pieces, things get a little more complicated. Their edges have to be precisely jointed. To joint

LAMINATE TRIMMER AND FLUSH-TRIMMING BIT JOINT VENEERS. To joint veneers for wide panels, the author uses a laminate trimmer (a small router) and a bearing-guided flush-trimming bit.

two sheets of veneer, I just sandwich them between two boards; the edge of the bottom board must be jointed and stick out ever so slightly (say, ¹⁄₃₂ in.) beyond the top board. When clamped together with both pieces of veneer between and their edges sticking out past the bottom board, jointing is a simple matter of routing. With a bearing-guided, flush-trimming bit, make a pass down the board, and that's that (see the photo above).

Use veneer tape (a water-activated adhesive tape available from veneer suppliers) to tape these jointed veneers together. Tape them along the seam on the face side. Then use a hot iron on the veneer tape to dry the tape and to shrink it a bit so the joint between the veneer sheets is very tight. The veneer will warp a bit from the iron's dry heat but not enough to matter when it goes into the vacuum press.

The last thing to do before glue-up is to mark each ply and sheet of veneer on one edge with a tick mark at the center to help align the layers on the form.

FOAM ROLLER SPREADS UREA FORMALDE-HYDE OR PLASTIC-RESIN GLUES EASILY. These two types of glue have longer set times than white or yellow glues, so they're better for most veneer work. A thin, even layer of glue on one of the surfaces is sufficient.

GLUE-UP

Next I glue up the stack of plies and veneer using a urea-formaldehyde or plastic-resin glue. I use these glues because of their longer open times compared to yellow glue and because they don't creep. The glue I use most often, Unibond 800 (available from Vacuum Pressing Systems, 553 River Road, Brunswick, ME 04011; 207-725-0935), also is available in different colors and can be dyed to make gluelines or squeeze-out less obvious. Unibond cleans up with warm water—not an easy thing to do with plastic-resin glues. And setup time can be modified by the application of heat and by the ratio of resin to hardener you use.

Apply either of these types of glue with a thin, foam-covered roller (available at most hardware and paint stores). A thin, even coat on one of the two surfaces will create a strong glue bond (see the photo above). Finally, after you've glued and stacked all the layers, use the tick marks on the veneer and substrate to align the stock correctly. Use masking tape to hold the stack together at the center on both sides.

INTO THE VACUUM BAG

Inside the vacuum bag, I use a melamine platen (a large, flat plate on which something is pressed). I cut ⅛-in.-wide, ⅛-in.-deep grooves with a table saw to make a grid of 6-in. squares on the platen, as recommended by the manufacturer. The platen is 2 in. to 4 in. larger than the base of the form, so there's plenty of bag to wrap around the form. The form goes in the bag and on the platen. I keep the form as close to the opening as possible to make it easier to put the lamination into the bag. I also roll up the unused end of the bag. That way, the vacuum pump doesn't have to work as hard at evacuating air from the bag initially, and the pump cycles on less often while the glue sets.

Now I put the laminations into the bag with waxed or paper-wrapped cauls top and bottom to ensure even pressure over the entire lamination. The edges of the form and of the cauls are rounded over so they don't puncture the bag. I usually duct-tape the whole lamination to the form at a center point I've marked on the form. The masking tape that I put on earlier over the center mark of the lamination locates its center. The duct tape keeps the lamination in place, but it still allows the plies to slide by each other as they get squished against the form.

Once I've closed the bag and started to pump out the air, I move quickly. It's important to make sure the bag isn't pinched between the form and platen, between lamination and form, or between layers of the lamination itself. If you do pinch the bag, you'll end up with a void in the lamination and a bump on its surface.

It's also essential to check that the bag is bearing against the entire lamination, that it isn't hung up anywhere (preventing it from contacting the lamination), and that the bag

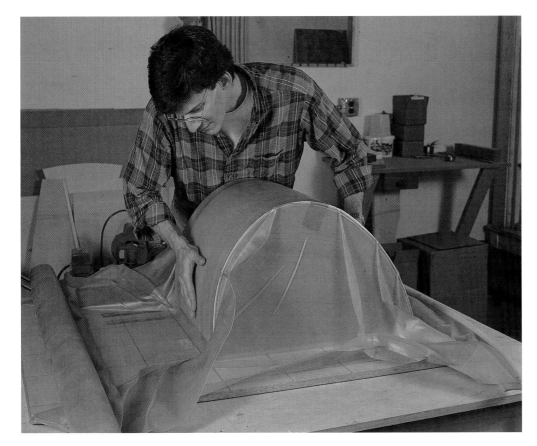

MAKE SURE THE BAG ISN'T PINCHED. Check that the bag isn't caught between layers of the lamination, the form, or the platen. There should be no air pockets between the bag and the lamination, which would mean a weak bond in that spot.

has been evacuated completely (see the photo above). Sometimes air pockets remain because the bag has closed off any exit channels, which can keep layers of the lamination from bonding. If I see any gaps between plies at the edges, I'll turn off the vacuum pump, open the bag, let some air in, close the bag, and start evacuating it again, taking more care to see that the bag seats flush against the entire lamination.

ELECTRIC BLANKET SPEEDS DRYING

To speed the glue-cure time once the lamination is under pressure, place an electric blanket, set on high, over the bag. This can reduce the cure time of the Unibond from about four hours to just over an hour. Electric blankets weren't designed to be

folded over a plastic bag, though, so don't leave the blanket on unattended.

I leave my glue-mixing stick underneath the blanket on top of the vacuum bag, and I set an inexpensive plastic thermometer next to it. By knowing the temperature just outside the bag and comparing this information with that provided by the manufacturer of the adhesive, I can get a rough idea of how long before the glue will be cured; then I can turn off the blanket and the vacuum pump. The reason for keeping the glue-mixing stick there is just to play it safe. It will show me for certain when the glue has cured. When the thin film of adhesive that remains on the mixing stick has turned brittle and dry, the lamination is ready.

PETER KORN

A Hall Table That's Both Traditional and Contemporary

I suspect I'm not the only one who's drawn to narrow tables that sit in a hall or behind a sofa. There is something inherently graceful in their spare form. And I'm a little nostalgic about a rosewood table—elegantly proportioned with a carved apron—that stood in my parents' home when I was growing up.

When I decided to build a hall table for my own home, I settled on a straightforward design. The table has an ebonized base and a top elevated above the base by an inch. Because it lacks carving, inlay, or other ornamentation, its success depends on the quality of the joinery, the surface preparation, and the finish.

I wanted to focus attention on the top. So by dyeing the base black, I made it recede visually, effectively bringing the top into the foreground. For the same reason, I recessed the top's connection to the base to create a floating effect. With all this emphasis on the top, you might expect that I would have used a highly figured, exotic wood. I didn't. I chose a relatively serene piece of cherry. As an object meant for daily domestic use, the table expresses the beauty of the ordinary. The quieter wood seemed to be more appropriate.

The base of the table is built entirely from 1¼-in.-sq. soft maple. It's assembled with 44 mortise-and-tenon joints, and where the lower aprons cross the inner legs, there are four half-lap joints, as shown in the top drawing on p. 82.

BUILDING THE BASE

Before building any project, I draw it out full-scale to clarify any complex joinery and prevent layout errors.

Because there are only four half-laps in the table, a combination of hand and machine work was the quickest and most enjoyable way to get excellent results. I made the half-laps by following the series of steps shown in the photos on p. 80. These half-laps add racking resistance and rigidity to the table.

I prefer handwork where appropriate, but faced with 44 identical mortises, I decided the better part of valor was to use my slot mortiser for these joints. A plunge router and mortising fixture also would work quite well.

To make the tenons, I cut the shoulders first with a sliding crosscut box on the table saw. Then I sawed the cheeks with a shop-made jig that holds the work vertically and slides along the rip fence. I completed the tenons by sawing them to width against a fence on the bandsaw.

The table's top is supported by two cross rails, which started out as 1¼-in. by 2¼-in. blanks. I bandsawed a 45-degree angle up

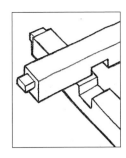

USE ONE PIECE TO MARK THE OTHER for a tight joint. Extend the layout lines halfway down each side to mark the sides of the joint.

TO AVOID TEAROUT, the author cuts a shallow groove on the waste side of the joint. The groove has one straight side at the shoulder.

DADO BLADE REMOVES BULK OF WASTE. The author uses two miter gauges screwed to a common fence for accuracy and stability. The dado blade is set to cut the full depth of the half-lap.

CHOP OUT REMAINING WASTE. The author starts paring the shoulder by using a mallet and a razor-sharp chisel that's narrower than the joint. He chops the waste from the center of the shoulder and then gradually pares to the outside edges.

from the rails' intersections with the upper aprons (see the top drawing on p. 82) to give the top the appearance of floating above the base.

To attach the top, I bored a single recessed hole (for a round-head screw and washer) in the center of each of the two support rails. Then I made a slotted screw hole near each end of the support rails. Slotted screw holes allow the top to expand and contract with changes in humidity. The fixed screws in the center of each rail ensure that any movement is divided equally between front and back.

I glued the base together in three stages, as explained in the bottom drawing on p. 82. I started with the inner legs, short center stiles, and the two aprons; finished up the front and rear assemblies; and finally, connected the front and rear assemblies with the short side pieces. Before each assembly, I scraped and sanded any faces that would be hard to reach later.

After the glue had set, I planed and scraped the joints flush. Once I had the base assembled and all joints flush, I sanded the whole assembly with 120-grit paper, wet the wood to raise the grain, then sanded again with 220-grit. I raised the grain because I used a water-based ani-line stain to ebonize the base, and I didn't want to sand through the stain to knock down the grain.

MAKING THE TOP

I assembled the top out of pieces cut from a single cherry board so that the color and grain would match well. By inserting a biscuit every 10 in. or so, I kept the joints in the top fairly flush during glue-up. After giving the glue a few hours to set up, I cut the top to width and length on the table saw, with a 15-degree bevel around the perimeter.

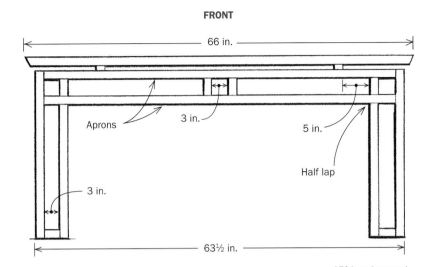

FRONT

66 in.

Aprons   3 in.   5 in.

Half lap

3 in.

63½ in.

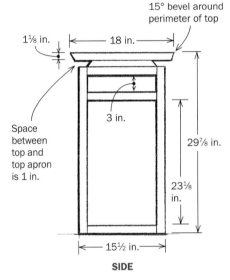

15° bevel around perimeter of top

1⅛ in.   18 in.

Base components are all 1¼ in. sq., except for a pair of cross rails that support the top. They are 1¼ in. by 2¼ in. A 1-in. space separates the top from the frame and helps focus attention on the top.

3 in.

Space between top and top apron is 1 in.

29⅞ in.

23⅛ in.

15½ in.

SIDE

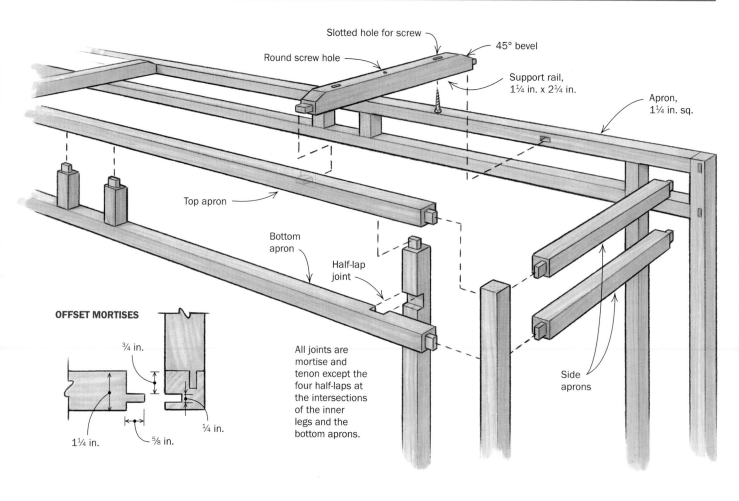

Slotted hole for screw

Round screw hole

45° bevel

Support rail,
1¼ in. x 2¼ in.

Apron,
1¼ in. sq.

Top apron

Bottom
apron

Half-lap
joint

OFFSET MORTISES

¾ in.

¼ in.

1¼ in.

⅝ in.

All joints are
mortise and
tenon except the
four half-laps at
the intersections
of the inner
legs and the
bottom aprons.

Side
aprons

■ **Gluing Up Parts**

This table is glued up in three
stages (each new step is shaded
in blue).

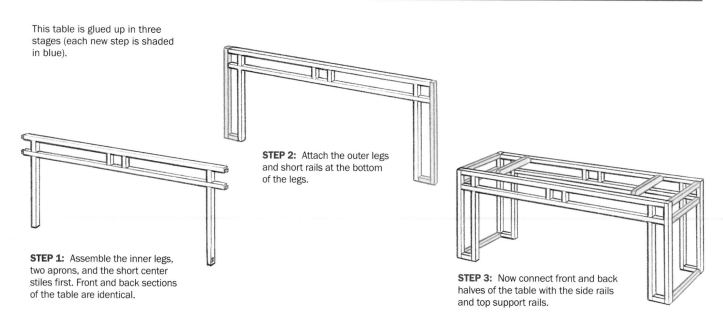

STEP 2: Attach the outer legs
and short rails at the bottom
of the legs.

STEP 1: Assemble the inner legs,
two aprons, and the short center
stiles first. Front and back sections
of the table are identical.

STEP 3: Now connect front and back
halves of the table with the side rails
and top support rails.

FINISH PREPARATION: PLANE, SCRAPE, AND SAND

Wood grain displays its greatest depth and clarity when it's been sliced cleanly with a sharp handplane. The surface of the wood reflects light straight back to the eye. Conversely, abrading wood can leave small scratches, which tend to dull or obscure the grain. This is especially true of coarser sandpaper, which can leave deep scratches that are difficult to eliminate.

Unfortunately, wood doesn't always respond cooperatively to planing. Knots, swirly grain, and figured lumber all present challenges that are far more easily addressed by scraping and sanding with fine sandpaper. The exact steps I take depend on the individual boards I'm working with, but generally, I'll start with a plane, proceed to a scraper, then sand with fine paper.

When planing a surface in preparation for a finish, I want the most polished surface I can get, so I adjust my smoothing plane's frog so that the mouth is just $\frac{1}{32}$ in. wide. Minimizing the opening greatly reduces the possibility of tearout. Also, by grinding the blade to a slightly convex shape, I don't leave edge marks on the wood, and I can prevent the corner of the blade from catching and gouging the surface.

For this tabletop, I followed up my planing by scraping the top and then sanding, beginning with 150-grit. I didn't scrape the underside, sides, or ends of the top—each for a different reason: the underside because I'm trying to get away from that level of preciousness in my work; the sides because the plane had already left them virtually perfect; and the ends because scraping end grain doesn't work well. I also sanded the bottom, sides, and ends with 150-grit. And I wet all the surfaces of the tabletop to raise the grain and then sanded with 220-grit.

FINISHING

I ebonized the base by applying several coats of black, water-soluble aniline dye. Because water raises the grain, it's a good idea to make a preemptive strike: Wet the table base with water a second time to raise the grain again, and then sand with 320-grit paper after the table has dried. After that, follow the manufacturer's instructions for mixing and applying the dye. It takes two or three coats, with drying time in-between, to get a rich, deep black.

After the wood was ebonized, I applied three coats of an oil and varnish mixture, applying the first coat with a cotton rag and then wiping it dry after a few minutes. I applied the second and the third coats in the same way, but I wet-sanded the second coat with a sheet of 400-grit wet-or-dry sandpaper and wet-sanded the third coat with a sheet of 600-grit.

Be careful not to sand the corners of the wood, or you could sand right through the stain. If this happens, the best solution is to touch-up the light spots with an indelible black magic marker. It works.

I used the same oil-and-varnish mixture on the cherry top. This finish doesn't offer the degree of protection from abrasion and liquids that a straight varnish would, but I prefer the look of an oil-and-varnish mixture. It dries in the wood, not on it, so the wood retains a seductive visual and tactile appeal.

PETER TURNER

Entertainment Center in Quartersawn Maple

As my 2-year-old daughter, Morrigan, grew and became more mobile and curious, so did the urgency to design and build an entertainment center. My aim was to keep the unit looking more like a piece of furniture than a refrigerator while efficiently housing the television, VCR, and other audio components out of sight and temptation's way.

In an effort to move away from the large, heavy look of a typical entertainment center, my first design ended up as a horizontal case on a skinny, four-legged frame. I eventually scrapped this design because I realized the weight of components, especially a television, would overwhelm such a delicate piece. Instead, the cabinet evolved into a more conventional two-piece structure, with a lower section housing three drawers for storage of CDs and tapes and a slightly narrower but taller upper section enclosed by a pair of doors. I did what I could to keep the piece from getting bulky by maximizing the usable internal space and adding soft curves to the exterior, which help mask its rather hefty dimensions.

I chose cranked door hinges that allow a door to be opened a full 270 degrees instead of pocket door hardware, which would have added several inches to the width of the piece. The curved legs lift the case off the floor and help reduce its visual weight. And to blend the lower case with the upper, I applied cove moldings at the waist and at the crown. I really like the

swoop of a cove, which lends vitality to a piece.

To ensure that components such as an amplifier, tuner, CD player, and a television would fit inside the upper cabinet, I took a tape measure to my electronic gear. I also checked the dimensions of stereo and TV components at an electronics store. New electronic components are fairly standardized, being about 17 in. wide or less and just a few inches tall. Older components vary more in size. I settled on four 18-in.-wide adjustable shelves that are shallower than the interior of the case, which allows room for routing wires and for air circulation. The cabinet will easily hold half a dozen components plus a 27-in. television. The back of the upper case has a panelless frame, which makes for easy access to wires and lets the heat produced by a television escape.

With the help of a friend, Sam Robinson, I built the cabinet within a narrow time frame—one month—because I wanted to exhibit the piece at the Philadelphia Furniture Show. Sam was assigned the upper case, and I took on the lower box. We kept our fingers crossed and hoped that the bridge would eventually meet in the middle.

Quartersawn maple is the predominant wood used in the piece. The wood was chosen for its light color and subtle grain. Soft maple was used for the drawer sides and

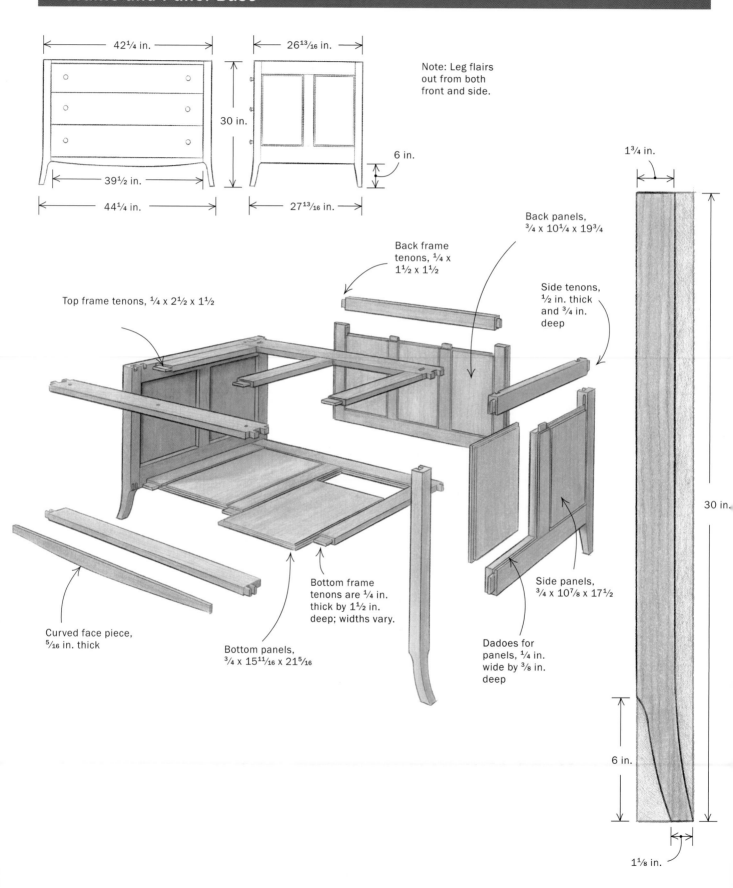

42¼ in.

26¹³⁄₁₆ in.

Note: Leg flairs out from both front and side.

30 in.

6 in.

39½ in.

44¼ in.

27¹³⁄₁₆ in.

1¾ in.

Back panels,
¾ x 10¼ x 19¾

Back frame
tenons, ¼ x
1½ x 1½

Side tenons,
½ in. thick
and ¾ in.
deep

Top frame tenons, ¼ x 2½ x 1½

30 in.

Side panels,
¾ x 10⅞ x 17½

Bottom frame
tenons are ¼ in.
thick by 1½ in.
deep; widths vary.

Dadoes for
panels, ¼ in.
wide by ⅜ in.
deep

Curved face piece,
⁵⁄₁₆ in. thick

Bottom panels,
¾ x 15¹¹⁄₁₆ x 21⁵⁄₁₆

6 in.

1⅛ in.

one internal frame. The drawer bottoms are made of plywood.

My local hardwood supplier, Dennis Day of Day Hardwoods in Scarborough, Maine, has a knack for finding high-quality wood at fair prices. He supplied me with 200 bd. ft. of quartersawn maple with several pieces close to 8 in. wide, unusually wide for quartersawn stock. The widest planks were used for visible panels and drawer fronts. The narrower stock was used for frames, internal panels, and shelves.

We were unable to locate thicker quartersawn stock, so we used plainsawn 16/4 material when needed, sawing it to best show off the grain.

THE STOUTEST TIMBERS ARE USED IN THE LOWER CASE

I rough-cut the 16/4 stock and let it sit a few days to stabilize. It seemed as if this big plank was custom-made for my purposes. I was able to get quartersawn boards for the side frames and coves. The rest of the plank had diagonal end grain, which was used for the legs. Diagonal end grain is ideal for legs because you can orient the stock to show rift-sawn figure on the two exposed faces.

I rough-cut the front legs about 3 in. square; the rear legs were roughed in at 2 in. by 3 in. The flat, inside faces of the legs were mortised to receive the side rails. I used a multirouter to cut all of my lower case joinery. Dadoes were routed into the legs for the panels. I cut the feet on the bandsaw and cleaned them up with a cabinet scraper (see the left photo below).

The back, top, and bottom frames are of mortise-and-tenon construction with routed stopped dadoes for all panels. Double dovetail joints were used to join the top frame to the rest of the lower case (see the right photo below). I used double tenons on the front corners of the bottom frame to reinforce these joints (see the center photo below). Single tenons are adequate at the rear of the case because the back provides additional strength.

The panels were rabbeted along all four exterior edges. The reveal between the panel and frame is slight, about 1/16 in. at the top and bottom and a hair more along the sides. To simplify production, I rabbeted all panels using the same setting. Next, I machined the dadoes in the frames, making them all 1/4 in. wide and 3/8 in. deep. Then I placed slivers of neoprene in the lower rails, which lift the panels to the correct height. Neoprene is available from window-repair companies.

The dry assembly of the lower case was my first opportunity to appreciate the real scale of the piece. I clamped a temporary spacer across the front between the upper corners of the sides to hold them in place. I then placed the completed top frame on top of the case and knifed the dovetail

AFTER CUTTING THE MORTISES, SHAPE THE FEET. The feet are cut out on the bandsaw, then cleaned up with a scraper.

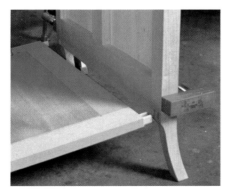

DOUBLE TENONS JOIN THE BOTTOM TO THE FRONT OF THE LOWER CASE. A single tenon is sufficient for the rear because the glued-in back panel will add strength.

THE TOP OF THE LOWER CASE IS A SIMPLE FRAME WITHOUT PANELS. Double dovetail joints are used at each corner to ensure the case won't bow.

UPPER AND LOWER CASES CAN BE SEPARATED FOR EASE IN MOVING. Threaded inserts and bolts are hidden from view but make a strong connection.

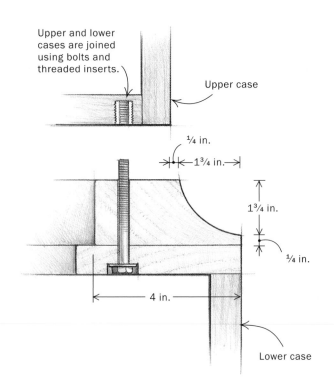

Upper and lower cases are joined using bolts and threaded inserts.

Upper case

¼ in.

1¾ in.

1¾ in.

¼ in.

4 in.

Lower case

WAIST MOLDING

Pairs of biscuits are used to join parts. The assembly is glued directly to the lower case.

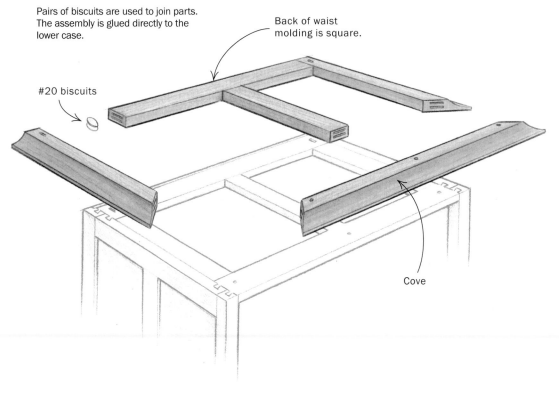

Back of waist molding is square.

#20 biscuits

Cove

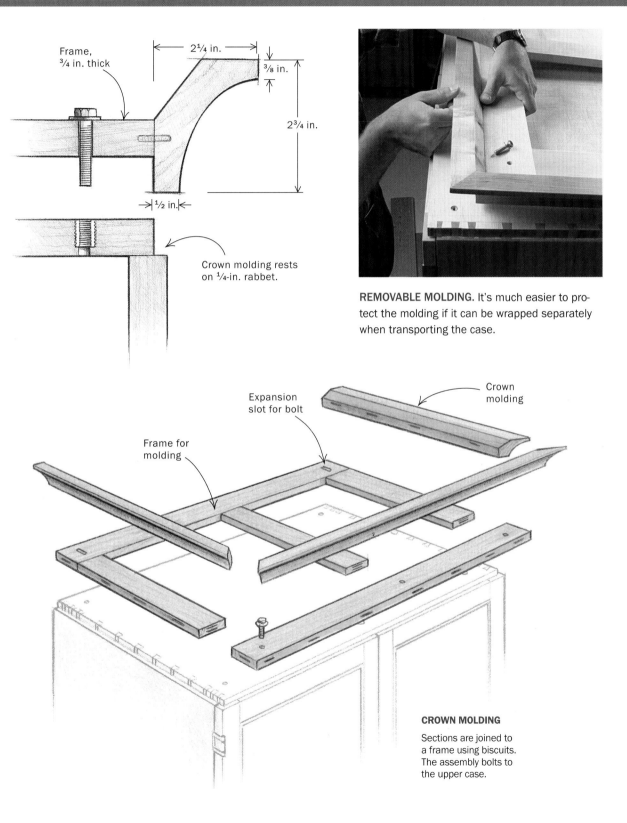

Frame,
³/₄ in. thick

2¹/₄ in.

³/₈ in.

2³/₄ in.

¹/₂ in.

Crown molding rests
on ¹/₄-in. rabbet.

REMOVABLE MOLDING. It's much easier to protect the molding if it can be wrapped separately
when transporting the case.

Crown
molding

Expansion
slot for bolt

Frame for
molding

CROWN MOLDING

Sections are joined to
a frame using biscuits.
The assembly bolts to
the upper case.

socket placement into the leg tops and upper rails.

After knocking the sides apart, I finished cutting the joinery. Then I glued it together. The back is handplaned to fit. It is glued in place.

A waist molding, built as an open framework, separates the top from the bottom half of the case. Three sides are shaped; the

SOURCES OF SUPPLY

DRAWER SLIDES

Julius Blum
7733 Old Plank Rd.
Stanley, NC 28164
800-438-6788

Hettich America
6225 Shiloh Rd.
Alpharetta, GA 30202
800-438-8424

HINGES

Hafele
3901 Cheyenne Dr.
Archdale, NC 27263
336-889-2322

Sugatsune America
221 E. Selandia Lane
Carson, CA 90746
800-562-5267

CRANKED HINGES ALLOW DOORS TO OPEN WIDE. Mortises must be cut in the doors and the front edge of the case.

back is square. I cut the cove molding on the table saw with the blade at 90 degrees, using a 25-degree angle of approach and ending up with a final blade height of 1½ in. I ran the stock facedown to provide a stable riding surface. Small, successive cuts with a grazing final pass are the keys to producing a clean cove safely. No matter how carefully you cut, there's still a bit of cleanup required. I made a custom scraper by grinding a stock scraper to the same radius as the cove. The front corners of the cove were mitered, and the rear corners were butt-joined. I used double #20 biscuits to reinforce all of the corner joints. The completed framework was glued directly to the top of the lower case. Biscuits are not needed here because there is plenty of face grain between parts.

HIDDEN, FULL-EXTENSION DRAWER SLIDES ARE USED

The three drawer boxes are all the same size and were built using a Leigh® dovetail jig. The drawer fronts were screwed in place from the inside. For visual balance, I graduated the height of the false fronts, with the lower drawer front being the deepest. After cutting all of the dovetail joints, I machined dadoes in the fronts and sides of each drawer for the plywood bottom panel, which is rabbeted along three edges. Then I ripped the bottom inch from each drawer back to allow the bottom panels to extend past the rear edge of the drawer. The bottoms were screwed in place to the rear drawer wall.

I also cut grooves in the front and rear of the upper drawer to hold removable partitions, good for CDs or tapes. The partitions are ¼ in. thick by 4 in. high, and they divide the drawer into six equal channels. I cut these after cutting the dovetails and dadoes. I clamped matching fronts and backs flat on my bench, butting their top edges together. Then, starting in the dado, I routed rounded, ⅛-in.-deep dadoes across both pieces using a ¼-in. core-box bit. After a little trial and error, I cut the partitions to length and rounded over the ends to match the round-bottomed dadoes. I carried the same profile along the top edge. Round dadoes are time-consuming, but I much prefer their softer look. Depending on the size of your CD or tape collection, other drawers could also be partitioned.

I chose Hettich International's® Quadro 30 V6 full-extension slides for their ease of installation, smooth operation, and clean look. Each drawer gets a pair of slides, which are screwed to the inside of the case. Two plastic clips, which engage the slides, are screwed to the underside of each drawer near the front. Drawers must be constructed so that their sides project ½ in. deeper than the drawer bottom. The slides are completely hidden by the drawer sides. With this type of hardware, I don't have to worry about whether my drawers will bind in the humid summer heat or get sloppy in the dry air of winter. I particularly like the self-closing action, which kicks in when a drawer is open an inch or less. Blum also makes a hidden drawer slide called the Tandem.

To locate each pair of drawer slides uniformly within the case, I made a spacing guide out of scrap plywood (see the top photo at right). Here's how it works: Lay out the location of the slides. Then trim the guide so that when placed inside the case, the slide, when laid on top of the guide, is in position for attachment to the case. The guide ensures that the opposite slide will be at the same level and parallel to the first. Start with the top drawer and cut the guide down for each subsequent pair of slides.

If you use Hettich slides, order their screws, too, which cost extra. I didn't and discovered that standard round-head screws interfered with the action of the slides. To finish off the lower case, I drilled ½-in.-deep mortises for the pulls, then attached the drawer fronts to the drawers with counter-sunk screws.

I added a curved face piece to the outside edge of the bottom of the case, below the last drawer, which helps tie the case to the curve of the legs. This face piece is glued in place. The pulls are classic Shaker design and made of ebony. The pulls for the upper case have soft tips to prevent dinging the case (see the photos and story on p. 95).

A SPACING GUIDE SIMPLIFIES THE INSTALLATION OF SLIDES. The guide positions each pair of slides at the correct height for attachment to the inside of the case. Cut the guide down to attach the next pair of slides.

REMOVABLE DIVIDERS MAKE THE DRAWERS VERSATILE. Whether you need to store CDs, tapes, or videocassettes, the drawers can accommodate all.

A FIXED SHELF AND CENTER DIVIDER STRENGTHEN THE UPPER CASE. Both the shelf and divider fit into ⅛-in.-deep stopped dadoes. The protruding ears at the front of the shelf and divider are dovetailed.

MARK THE SOCKET OF THE DOVETAILED EARS DURING DRY-FITTING. Clamp the case flat and use a sharp marking knife.

MEANWHILE, THE UPPER CASE IS TAKING SHAPE

While I was busy cutting mortises and tenons, Sam was working away at the long rows of half-blind dovetails that join the upper case. Once he finished the dovetails, he loaded the stock into his van and came to my shop for a dry assembly and test fit. We knocked his case together and placed it on top of my lower unit. Amazingly enough, it sat nice and flat with appropriate reveals on all sides.

The upper case has a fixed shelf, which fits into a ⅛-in.-deep stopped dado (see the photo above). The front of the fixed shelf has two ½-in.-deep ears, which are dovetailed into the front edge of the cabinet. The dovetails prevent the case from bowing. A center divider was attached to the case in a similar fashion, using dadoes and dovetailed ears. To place the sockets for the

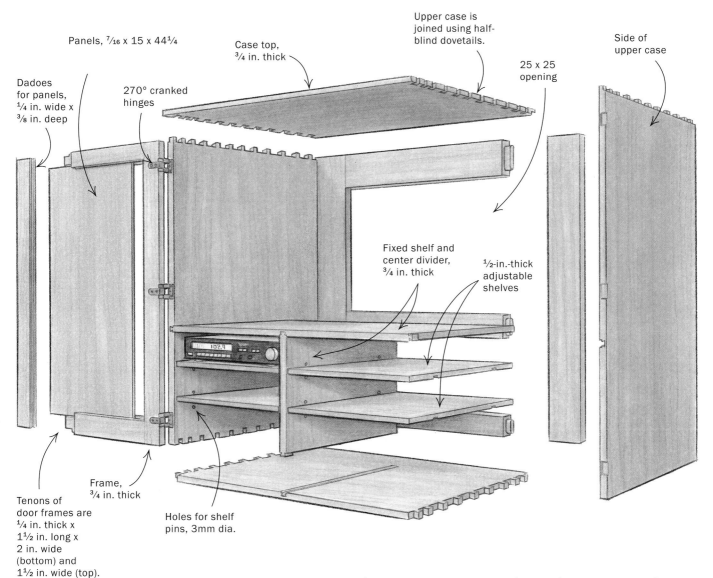

Panels, $^7/_{16}$ x 15 x 44$^1/_4$

Dadoes for panels, $^1/_4$ in. wide x $^3/_8$ in. deep

270° cranked hinges

Case top, $^3/_4$ in. thick

Upper case is joined using half-blind dovetails.

25 x 25 opening

Side of upper case

Fixed shelf and center divider, $^3/_4$ in. thick

$^1/_2$-in.-thick adjustable shelves

Tenons of door frames are $^1/_4$ in. thick x 1$^1/_2$ in. long x 2 in. wide (bottom) and 1$^1/_2$ in. wide (top).

Frame, $^3/_4$ in. thick

Holes for shelf pins, 3mm dia.

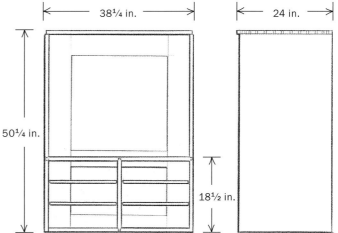

38$^1/_4$ in.

24 in.

50$^1/_4$ in.

18$^1/_2$ in.

dovetailed ears accurately, it's best to dry-fit the case with the shelf and divider and mark out their locations with a knife (see the bottom photo on the facing page).

Back at his shop, Sam chopped out the sockets. He also attached threaded inserts into the case. The inserts, in conjunction with bolts, allow the upper and lower cases to be joined. The crown molding was also attached in this way.

DON'T COME UNHINGED BECAUSE OF HARDWARE

Sam built the door frames using haunched mortise-and-tenon joints. Panels were constructed using the same methods employed in the lower case. The hinge mortises were marked using a knife, then most of the waste was removed by routing freehand. A chisel and gouge finished the mortises.

We used Hafele hinges (No. 307.04.806) and ran into a few bumps along the way. Because I wanted the doors to be flush to the sides of the case, we mortised the hinges into the outside edges of the doors. As designed, the hinges require that a door be inset from the side of the case by half the thickness of the hinge. When we hung the doors, they didn't swing open all of the way.

First, we thought it was because we had modified the hardware installation. But as it turned out, the problem was with the thickness of the doors. For these hinges to work properly, the doors need to be a hair under ¾ in. thick, or ⁴⁷⁄₆₄ in. thick, to be exact. We also discovered that the hinges didn't close properly through no fault of our own. We removed them after a trial fit and found that the hinges were not manufactured perfectly square. We fixed them with a hammer and vise.

After the doors were planed to fit, Sam drilled the mortises for the knobs, which are located at the level of the interior fixed shelf. He also drilled the 3mm-dia. holes in the sides of the case and center divider for Hafele shelf pins (No. 282.06. 500). I like these brass pins, which are round and stepped from 3mm dia. to 5mm. dia. Typical shelf pins require larger-diameter holes, 5mm or ¼ in., and it's surprising how discreet the 3mm holes are. Finally, Sam routed short recesses into the shelf bottoms to house the pins and keep the shelves from sliding.

THE CROWN MOLDING IS BOLTED IN PLACE

We designed the crown molding as a frame and made it detachable, which comes in handy when the case has to be moved. Sam cut the molding on his table saw in two steps.

The lower section of the molding has a bigger radius than the upper sweep. The lower radius was done with a 33-degree angle of approach with a final blade height of ½ in. The upper radius was done with a 21-degree angle of approach with a ⁹⁄₁₆-in. final blade height. Then Sam blended the transition between the two radii by moving the fence and blade and setting it by trial and error. A scraper was used to clean up the saw marks.

The crown was mitered at the front corners, and butt joints were used elsewhere. Pairs of #20 biscuits were used at all of the joints. The entire frame slips down over the case and rests on a rabbet cut into the sides. This rabbet was cut with a router after the upper case was assembled. Bolts and threaded inserts hold the molding in place.

To finish this cabinet, we sanded up to 220 grit, then wiped everything down with a damp cloth to raise the grain. Once the piece was dry, we finish-sanded to 320 grit.

Most of the case was finished with three coats of Bartley gel varnish. We chose this finish because it can be applied by hand, has good durability, and does not yellow maple as many oil finishes do. The insides of the lower case and the drawers were finished using extra blond shellac. Last, we attached the knobs, and before the epoxy had set, the entertainment center was inside my van, on its way to the Philadelphia Furniture Show.

PULLS THAT WON'T DING THE CASE

A door that swings on a 270-degree cranked hinge is great for access but can be hard on the case. That's because the pulls will smack into the side of the cabinet. To prevent dings I added nearly invisible neoprene bumpers to the upper pulls.

After turning a pull, I drilled a shallow hole in the tip. Using a leather punch the same diameter as the hole, I punched out a disc of black neoprene. The disc was pressed in place. I added a drop of cyanoacrylate glue to help keep it there. The protruding neoprene was trimmed flush using a sharp chisel. Because the pulls contact the sides in a direct line, not at an angle, the neoprene won't leave scuff marks.

DRILL A SHALLOW HOLE IN THE TIP OF THE PULL. The author uses a ¼-in. brad-point drill bit fitted to a chuck in the lathe's tailstock.

PUNCH OUT A NEOPRENE PLUG. Use a leather punch the same diameter as the hole in the pull.

PRESS THE NEOPRENE INTO THE TIP OF THE PULL. Use cyanoacrylate glue and then trim off the excess, using a sharp chisel.

LINDSAY SUTER

Joinery for Light, Sturdy Coffee Table

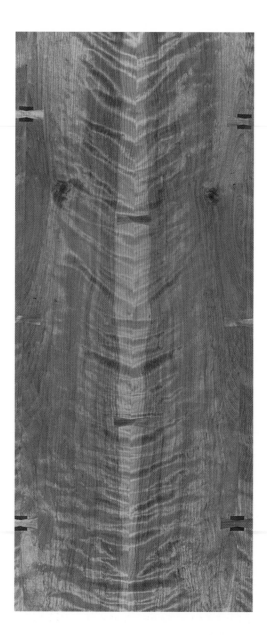

I knew a wood supplier in California, a whacky old hippie, whose joy was salvaging trees everyone else overlooked and then turning the wood into spectacular lumber. His lumberyard may have been in complete chaos, but he had a gift for finding the raw material for truly memorable furniture. It was in these wood stacks that I found the curly cherry perfectly suited for a low coffee table I had designed.

The table looks quite simple, but its exposed joinery puts craftsmanship as well as the figured wood on display. Through tenons, wedged with butterfly keys, join the legs to the top. Narrow stretchers replace more traditional aprons, keeping the table looking light and airy. The design also is a little daring because the tabletop is fastened directly to the legs.

I wondered as I drew up the plans whether this feature might result in a split top. As it turns out, the frame of this table flexes slightly as the top expands and contracts across its width. This is a result of using relatively thin stretchers, only ½ in. thick, that are set well below the top of the frame. Because the frame isn't absolutely rigid, the top has enough freedom of movement so it won't split. I know because the first one I made went to a client in Massachusetts where summers are hot and humid and indoor winter con-

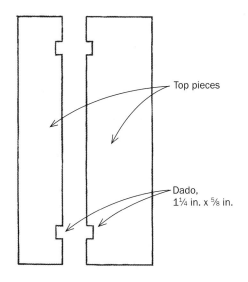

Top pieces

Dado,
1¼ in. x ⅝ in.

**MORTISES ON THE TABLE
SAW.** The tabletop mortises
are cut with a dado blade and
a crosscut sled. Mating boards
are clamped face to face
against the sled's fence.

ditions are bone dry. The table has been there for seven years and shows no sign of a problem. Even so, I would choose a relatively stable wood for this design. Quartersawn white oak, nara, or myrtle wood all seem like good choices to me.

CUTTING MORTISES WITH A DADO BLADE

The top was glued up from four bookmatched pieces that give the table a symmetrical quality. The leg tenons penetrate the top at the two outside joint lines. The inlaid butterfly keys let into the tops of the legs not only reinforce the joints between the top boards but also wedge the leg tenons. Cutting mortises into the tabletop where the boards are joined simplifies construction.

I cut the mortises with a dado blade and a crosscut sled on the table saw before gluing the top pieces together (see the photo above). After testing the setup on a piece of scrap, I can complete the mortises in a couple of passes.

I used dowels to align and register the edge-glued top joints. I marked the location of the butterfly keys first, so I didn't end up with a dowel in the way later on. To give the top a light, thin appearance without compromising its strength, I tapered the underside of the top at the edge. I used a tall auxiliary fence clamped to the table saw's rip fence with the blade fully raised and tilted away from the fence at about 5 degrees. The fence is positioned about ⅜ in. away from the blade, and the top is run through the saw on edge. A featherboard helps hold the top against the fence.

TENONED, MORTISED, AND TAPERED LEGS

There are four steps in making the simple, tapered legs: sizing the stock, cutting the tenons, cutting the mortises, and tapering the inside faces. Cutting the joints is much easier while the stock is still square. Leave the leg stock slightly long so there will be an extra ⅟₁₆ in. or so of the tenon protruding through the top. Although the tenon will be sanded or planed flush later, the result is a cleaner finished joint.

To prepare a tenon for a wedge, I drill a hole just above the tenon's shoulder, so the wedge won't split the leg. Then I bandsaw a kerf down the tenon to the hole. Remember to orient the leg wedges so that they run perpendicular to the grain of the tabletop, not with it.

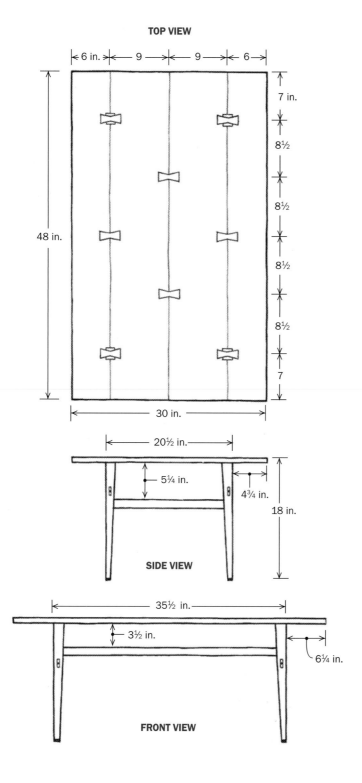

TOP VIEW

←6 in.→ ←— 9 —→ ←— 9 —→ ←— 6 —→

7 in.

8½

8½

8½

8½

7

48 in.

30 in.

←— 20½ in. —→

5¼ in.

4¾ in.

18 in.

SIDE VIEW

←———— 35½ in. ————→

3½ in.

6¼ in.

FRONT VIEW

Before cutting the mortises for the stretchers, I mark each leg so I know where it belongs on the table and which faces are on the outside. Then I lay out the mortises on all the legs. I cut the mortises on a slot mortiser, but a router, drill press, or mallet and chisel will work equally well.

I taper the legs on the table saw, using a shop-built jig, a rectangular piece of plywood cut into an L shape. After double-checking that I'm tapering the inside faces of the legs, I run the jig along the fence of the table saw with the leg snugly seated in the jig. The offcuts are handy for cutting the stretcher shoulders to the angle of the legs.

I rescued some small scraps of ebony for the feet. The ¼-in.-thick ebony wears like iron and visually punctuates the ends of the tapered legs. I cut and glue the foot to the bottom of the leg and then countersink a screw for good measure.

LAY OUT STRETCHERS FROM THE LEGS

I measure and mark the stretchers by dry-fitting the legs into the top and clamping the stretcher in position at the correct height against the back of the legs. I leave a little extra length at both ends so the tenons will protrude through the legs and can be sanded flush later. I use the tapered, inside edge of the leg as a guide to scribe the shoulder line on the stretcher.

To cut the tenon with an angled shoulder, I use a tenoning jig on the table saw. Instead of clamping the stretcher in a vertical position, I back it up with an offcut from tapering the legs. This ensures the angle of the shoulder will match the angle of the tapered leg. As before, I clean up, pare and fit the tenons, then drill and kerf them for wedges.

BUTTERFLY-MORTISE JIG, made of plywood, is cut to shape and glued back together.

ASSEMBLE THE FRAME IN TWO STEPS

Before assembling the table, I make plenty of wedges from stock that's strong, straight grained, and contrasting in color to accent the joint. I also scrape and sand all the parts. Then I glue up two sets of legs to the long stretchers only. After applying glue to the leg-stretcher joints, I fit the joints firmly and set them with a wedge. Then, immediately, I set the assembly into the tabletop (without glue). This holds everything in the correct position.

After the glue has cured, I repeat the procedure with the shorter end stretchers. When these are dry, I glue and wedge the leg/stretcher assembly to the top. I use the top wedges to keep the leg tenons tight in the top until the butterfly keys are finally put into place. When the glue is fully cured, I sand the tenons and wedges flush with the legs and the top.

A JIG SIMPLIFIES THE BUTTERFLY KEYS

When making multiple, identical butterfly joints, I like to cut all the mortises with a jig first and then fit the butterflies to the mortises. I make the butterflies with a slight taper on the sides, which helps ensure a tight fit and keeps the leg tenons tight in the top.

ALIGN BUTTERFLY-MORTISING JIG WITH LAYOUT LINES. The rounded corners left by the router bit in the butterfly mortises are cleaned out with a chisel.

The Butterfly Keys

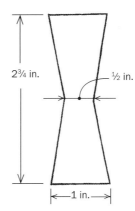

2¾ in.

½ in.

1 in.

The butterfly jig is a rectangular piece of ¾-in.-thick plywood cut into three sections. I cut the center section with a chop saw to shape the butterfly (see the left photo on p. 99). The pieces are glued back together, and centerlines are drawn to help with registration.

I lay out the centerlines for all the butterfly locations on the tabletop. Long layout lines make it easier to align the jig on the tabletop (see the right photo on p. 99). After clamping the jig securely in place, I rout the mortises with a flush-trimming, bearing-guided bit to a depth of about ⁷⁄₁₆ in. To complete the mortises, I clean up the corners with a chisel. I mill the butterfly stock to ½ in. thick and use the mortising jig to mark out the butterflies. After I bandsaw them to shape, I fit each butterfly, carving a slight taper on the sides. Each butterfly and its corresponding mortise are numbered.

I glue and clamp the butterflies in place, spreading the glue completely but sparingly, on the taper and on the bottom of the butterfly. I use deep-throated clamps and waxed blocks between joint and clamp. The blocks spread the clamp pressure over the whole butterfly and protect it from damage; the wax keeps the block from being glued to the top. The center butterflies can be tapped into place with a hammer and a block of wood while supporting the top from below. Or they can be clamped with battens above and below the table with clamps at either side.

When the glue has dried, I use a sharp jack plane to level the protruding butterflies with the tabletop. Then I sand the top, starting with 120-grit sandpaper, progressing up to 320-grit.

FINISH UP WITH OIL AND VARNISH

My favorite finish is a progressive buildup of four or five coats, starting with a straight oil finish, such as Watco®. With each successive coat, I add a little semigloss varnish and mineral spirits in equal parts until the mix consists of approximately one-third of each ingredient.

This finish gives a soft, lustrous surface with better wear resistance than straight oil. After the final coat is dry, I wax and lightly buff the entire piece with #0000 steel wool and then polish with a soft cloth.

A LOW COFFEE TABLE MAKES THE MOST OF WILDLY FIGURED WOOD. Mortises are cut in the top before glue-up.

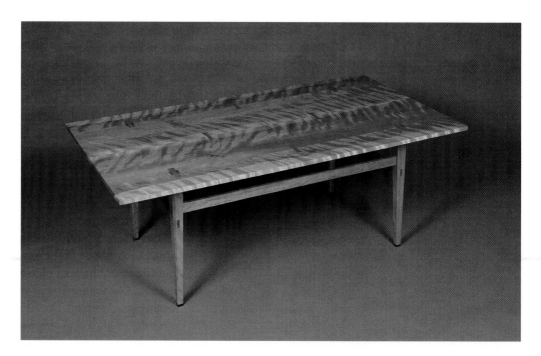

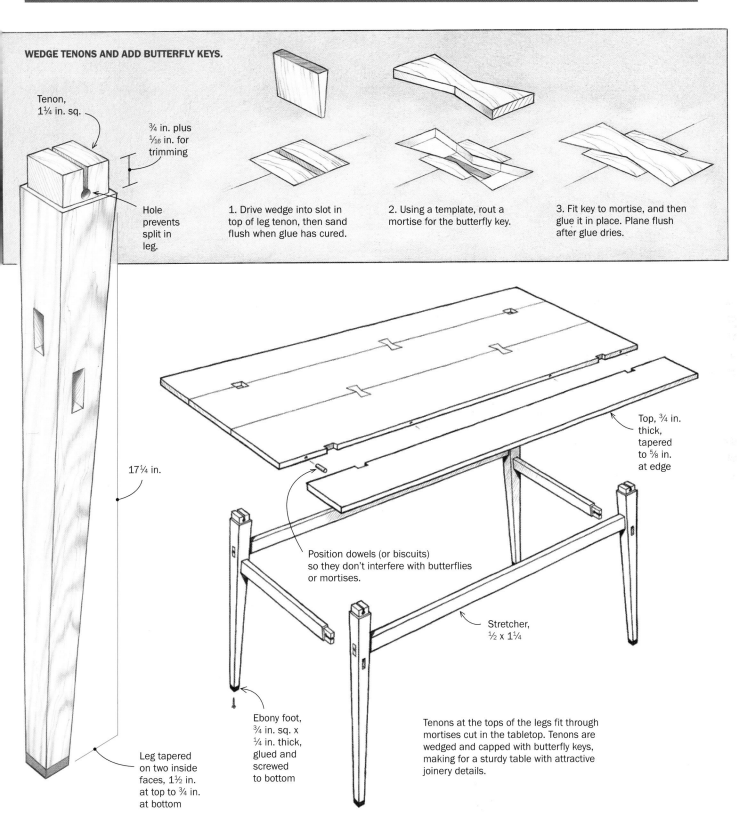

WEDGE TENONS AND ADD BUTTERFLY KEYS.

Tenon,
1¼ in. sq.

¾ in. plus
¹⁄₁₆ in. for
trimming

Hole
prevents
split in
leg.

1. Drive wedge into slot in top of leg tenon, then sand flush when glue has cured.

2. Using a template, rout a mortise for the butterfly key.

3. Fit key to mortise, and then glue it in place. Plane flush after glue dries.

17¼ in.

Top, ¾ in. thick, tapered to ⅝ in. at edge

Position dowels (or biscuits) so they don't interfere with butterflies or mortises.

Stretcher,
½ x 1¼

Ebony foot,
¾ in. sq. x
¼ in. thick,
glued and
screwed
to bottom

Leg tapered on two inside faces, 1½ in. at top to ¾ in. at bottom

Tenons at the tops of the legs fit through mortises cut in the tabletop. Tenons are wedged and capped with butterfly keys, making for a sturdy table with attractive joinery details.

M. FELIX MARTI

Shelving, Plain and Simple

A VERSATILE DESIGN FOR A VARIETY OF USES. These shelves can be sized to fit any location.

As unassuming as these shelves are, they have many of the features that I like most in furniture. They're lightweight, sturdy, and use simple, effective joinery. The design I use evolved partly from childhood memories of shelves in our house and partly from the built-in storage-shelf system that I now install in houses. Plastic laminate glued to both sides of medium-density fiberboard (MDF) or particleboard makes the shelving stiff. Tight-fitting dado joints and front and rear uprights at right angles to each other make the assembly strong and resistant to racking.

LAMINATE SHELF STOCK FIRST, THEN CUT TO SIZE

I glue the plastic laminate to a sheet of ⅝-in. particleboard or MDF. Melamine could be a less expensive and, perhaps, a less stiff alternative, but I have not used it for my shelves. A cabinet-component manufacturer is a good source of laminated stock if you don't want to make it yourself.

With a new shopmade throat plate in my table saw, I cut the shelves to size, using a Forrest Duraline HI-A/T blade made specifically for cutting double-sided laminated stock (Forrest Manufacturing Co., Inc., 457 River Road, Clifton, NJ 07014; 800-733-7111). There is virtually no chipping on the down side of the shelf stock.

DADO MATERIAL FOR CORNER UPRIGHTS

I lay out the shelf spacing on a 9-in.-wide oak board. This width will yield four 2-in.-wide upright corner posts with allowance for kerfs and some cleanup. Using a ½-in. down-shear bit in my router and the jig shown in the drawing on p. 104, I plow ¼-in.-deep dadoes across the full 9-in. width. The down-shear bit makes a clean

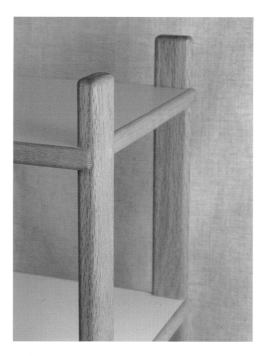

FRONT AND REAR UPRIGHTS, oriented at right angles to each other, provide lateral stability.

cut, and careful jig construction yields a dado so tight I have to tap the uprights onto the shelf stock. Then I rip this board into pieces a little wider than 2 in., which I feed on edge through a planer to produce uniform finished widths. Finally, I round over the corners and edges.

ASSEMBLE SHELVES AND UPRIGHTS

I now fit the shelf into the dadoes of the upright pieces so the shelf is flush with the edge of the upright. I drill through the corner uprights, using a tapered bit and counterbore. I use a 2-in. particleboard (not drywall) screw to fasten the pieces together. The deeper thread of the particleboard screw makes a strong joint. An oak plug glued into the counterbore finishes this simple connection.

To rout dadoes in stock for corner uprights, the author builds a jig to suit the exact shelf thickness. The stock is then ripped to width.

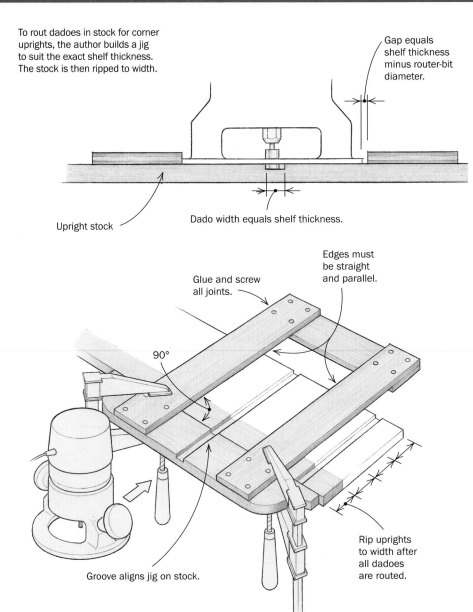

Gap equals shelf thickness minus router-bit diameter.

Dado width equals shelf thickness.

Upright stock

Edges must be straight and parallel.

Glue and screw all joints.

90°

Groove aligns jig on stock.

Rip uprights to width after all dadoes are routed.

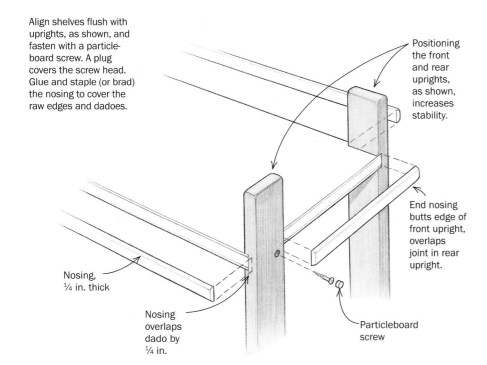

Align shelves flush with uprights, as shown, and fasten with a particle-board screw. A plug covers the screw head. Glue and staple (or brad) the nosing to cover the raw edges and dadoes.

Positioning the front and rear uprights, as shown, increases stability.

End nosing butts edge of front upright, overlaps joint in rear upright.

Nosing, ¼ in. thick

Nosing overlaps dado by ¼ in.

Particleboard screw

For the shelf-nosing stock, I plane a wide board a hair thicker than the thickness of the shelves and cut it to length. On my router table, I round over the ends and edges of this board for the front nosing and rip the rounded edge to a ¼-in. thickness. I round over this fresh edge on the router table and rip the next ¼-in. piece, alternating between router table and table saw until I have enough nosing for the job.

I glue and staple the nosing to the shelf edges, using a narrow-crown pneumatic stapler. The nosing is applied as shown in the drawing above. To me, the effect is a fully nosed shelf let into the uprights. A scraper flushes the nosing to the shelf surface. Using dry stock for the nosing guarantees that it won't shrink away from flush later.

By maintaining sharp planer knives and feeding stock slowly on the router table, I've just about eliminated any sanding. To complete the job, I apply a penetrating oil finish and fill the small wounds left by the staples with a crayon-type putty stick.

TRY DIFFERENT MATERIALS OR KNOCKDOWN CONSTRUCTION

I could get very different results by using the same basic idea and unusual materials. Marble or glass could be epoxied into dadoes in wood or metal uprights, or different woods could be used for the shelves and uprights (although I'd be concerned about shrinkage in the shelf thickness, which would reduce the effectiveness of the dado joint). For a knockdown version, I'd use threaded inserts in the shelves and machine screws instead of particleboard screws. Buttons would conceal the screws.

I'm pleased with the low cost, appearance, and strength of these units—happily, so is my wife, who has surrounded her weaving studio with them.

GARY ROGOWSKI

Gate-Leg Table Is Light but Sturdy

I was shown a picture once of a gate-leg dining table. It had eight cabriole legs, and it looked like an insect with a table-top on it. I delicately convinced my prospective clients to let me design a table with a little more grace that still had the drop leaves and gates they wanted. The tabletop was to be an oval large enough to seat eight comfortably. My concern was to lighten the base visually and still provide adequate support for the leaves. The table that resulted satisfied my clients' needs for utility and complemented its surroundings well.

Gate-leg tables were designed to save space. A leg-and-apron assembly, or gate, hinged to the table or pivoting on pins set into the table's framework, swings out to support a leaf that's hinged to the tabletop. In this way, a small table can be transformed easily into a larger one. A single gate can support a leaf on a smaller table, or double gates can be used for larger leaves, such as on this dining table. The gates can also be on one or both sides of the table, depending on the function of the table and how much extra space is desired. When not in use, two leaves take up hardly more space than one. For the finest appearance, rule joints are used between the leaves and top. This joint looks clean and provides support for the leaves.

Double gates can pivot either toward or away from each other. I decided to have the gates pivot away from each other so that with the leaves down, the gate legs would sit side by side. Measured together, the pair of gate legs are 2½ in. wide, or the same width as one of the outer table legs. This lightens the table visually by making it look like there's only one leg in the center of the table rather than two.

JOINERY AND PIVOTS

The table is made of cherry. I used 12/4 stock for the legs to avoid laminating thinner stock to get the 2½ in. I wanted. Crosscutting something this thick can be a problem. A 2½-in. leg is too thick for a 10-in. table-saw blade when the leg is riding in a crosscut carriage with a ¾-in. base. I got around this by using two miter gauges with a fence screwed on between them. With this two-miter-gauge setup, I can cut all the way through the legs in one pass. The two gauges also minimize any side-to-side slop that might occur with just one gauge, and the long, wooden fence between the two gauges lets me clamp a stop to it to index the length of my cuts for accurate multiple cuts.

DRILL BIT MARKS PIVOT POINT. After trimming pivot posts to size and checking the fit of the gates, the author marks where he'll drill for the bushing and hinge pin. He drops a drill bit through the bronze bushing in the rail to make a mark.

A HACKSAW BLADE MAKES QUICK WORK OF AN OVER-LONG BUSHING. With his drill press set at its lowest speed, the author makes two ½-in. bushings from one 1-in. bushing. It's easy to tell when you're through the bushing because sawdust from the dowel starts coming off the blade.

I used mortise-and-tenon construction for all the joinery on this table, routing the mortises and cutting the tenons on my table saw. The jigs I used for these two operations are as simple as could be, but they do their jobs well and take practically no time to make (see the sidebar on p. 112).

The leaves needed to fold down without binding on the top of the gate. For this to work out, the gates had to pivot out of the way into the table base itself (see the drawing on p. 110).

After cutting, routing, and dry-fitting all the joinery, I cut notches in the top and bottom rails where the gate legs will nest, dadoing them just ¾ in. deep. Keeping the dadoes this shallow ensured I didn't weaken the rails. It also meant I'd have to notch the legs later, so they'd tuck into the rails inside the plane of the table's outer legs. I made the notches in the rail a little wider than the combined width of the two gate legs to allow for the swing of the legs as they open and close.

I debated between using wooden dowels or steel pins for hinging the gates and ended up opting for the steel pins, which I set in bronze bushings. This choice allowed me to deal with glue-ups with something approaching leisure, letting me add on the two gate assemblies later. Another advantage of using steel pins and bronze bushings is that they will probably last through more than a few dinner parties.

I drilled the rails for the gate-pivot pins and bushings on my drill press. For the ½-in.-OD, ⅜-in.-ID bushings I found at my hardware store, I used a ½-in. brad-point bit and drilled exactly ½ in. into the rails. Next I centered a ¹³⁄₃₂-in. bit (⅜ in. was just a little too snug for the steel pins) on the dimple at the bottoms of the bushing holes in the rails and drilled all the way through the rails into scrap to prevent tearout. Then I took a smear of epoxy and glued the bushings into their holes in the rails.

The bushings were twice as long as I needed, so I came up with a simple, quick way of turning one into two. I marked the bushings with a pencil midway along their length, stuck a ⅜-in. dowel most of the way through the bushing and then chucked the dowel into the drill press.

I set my hacksaw on a wooden block and adjusted the drill-press table so that the hacksaw blade was even with the pencil mark and the blade's teeth face into the rotating bushing. I cut the bushing with the drill press set at its lowest speed (see the photo above). I could tell when I was through the bushing because the blade started spitting sawdust. I deburred the inner edges of the bushings before epoxying them into the legs and pivot posts.

As a last step before gluing, I dry-clamped each half of the base together to ensure that everything fit well. And then I marked and mitered the ends of the upper rail tenons on both the ends and sides.

GLUE-UP SEQUENCE

I glued the vertical columns to the long rails first, taking care to make sure that the frame went together perfectly square by temporarily dry-clamping the legs to the rails. Next I glued the long side rails to the legs. After that joint set up, I joined the two long assemblies with the short end rails. It helps not to be too liberal with the glue for the long side rails because you'll have the glue puddling up inside the mortise for the end rails. Then you'll have to wipe or chip the mess out.

I checked both gates as I was gluing them up to ensure they stayed flat, and I was careful not to overclamp. A twisted gate will cause major problems when you try to fit it to the table. I sighted across the posts and rails of the gate to see that they were in line. If they had been out of alignment, I would have used some judicious clamp-tweaking to pull them flat. After the gate assemblies had dried, I notched the gate-leg posts on the table saw so that they would mate with the notches on the rails and be out of the way of the leaves.

FITTING THE GATES

I set the two gate assemblies in place so that the center of the pivot posts lined up with the centers of the bushed holes in the rails. I trimmed the pivot posts as necessary to fit between the top and bottom rails without binding and without too much play. I also checked to ensure that the reveal between the gate legs was even top to bottom. Once I was satisfied with how the gates looked in relation to the rest of the table, I marked

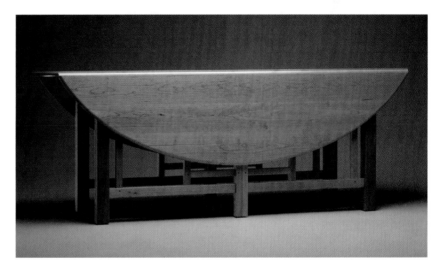

CONTEMPORARY LINES AND THIN GATE LEGS GIVE THIS TABLE A LIGHT FEEL (top). The table's size, 60 in. by 84 in., seats eight, but when the leaves are down, the table is more compact and can be moved against the wall for more floor space (bottom).

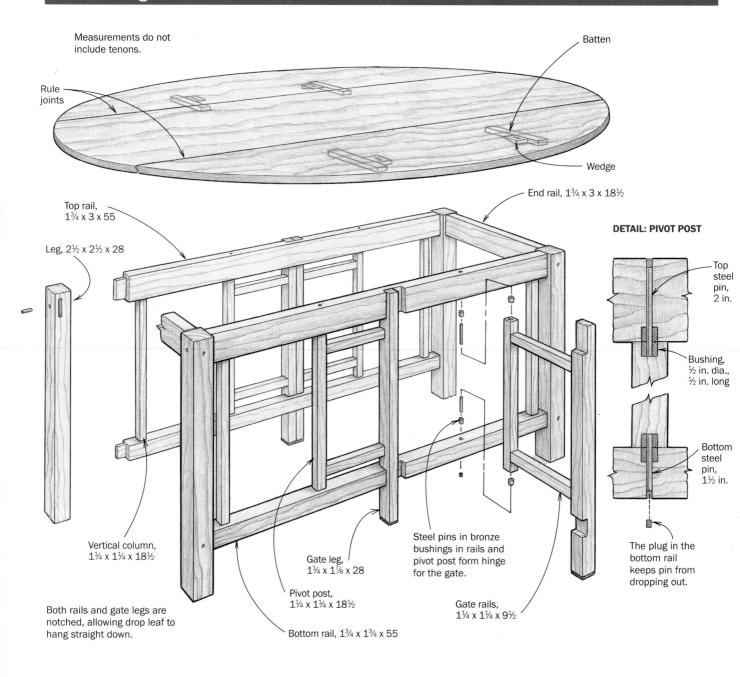

Measurements do not include tenons.

Batten

Rule joints

Wedge

End rail, 1¾ x 3 x 18½

Top rail, 1¾ x 3 x 55

DETAIL: PIVOT POST

Leg, 2½ x 2½ x 28

Top steel pin, 2 in.

Bushing, ½ in. dia., ½ in. long

Vertical column, 1¼ x 1¼ x 18½

Gate leg, 1¼ x 1⅛ x 28

Bottom steel pin, 1½ in.

Steel pins in bronze bushings in rails and pivot post form hinge for the gate.

Pivot post, 1¼ x 1¼ x 18½

The plug in the bottom rail keeps pin from dropping out.

Both rails and gate legs are notched, allowing drop leaf to hang straight down.

Gate rails, 1¼ x 1¼ x 9½

Bottom rail, 1¾ x 1¾ x 55

centers on the pivot posts by dropping a ⅜-in. bit down through the bushing in the top rail and pushing it up through the bushing in the bottom rail (see the photo on p. 107). Then I just repeated the procedure I went through for the rails on the pivot posts, drilling for the bushing first and then for the steel pin. I plugged the hole in the bottom of the bottom rail later

to keep the pin from dropping out with the gate attached to the base.

I also slightly beveled the insides of the outer gate legs where they come together, so they wouldn't bind when both were opened together. Then I marked and trimmed the bottoms of the legs so that with plastic glides on them, they're just touching the floor. If the legs are too short, they won't

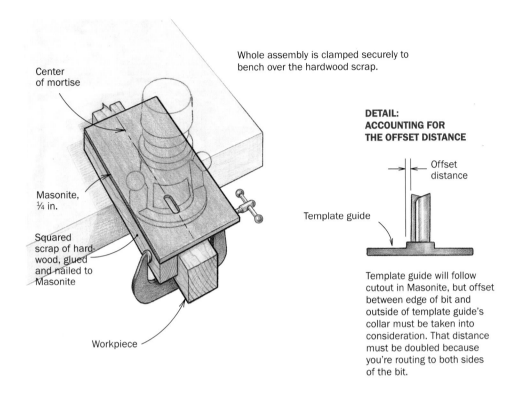

Center of mortise

Whole assembly is clamped securely to bench over the hardwood scrap.

Masonite, ¼ in.

Squared scrap of hardwood, glued and nailed to Masonite

Workpiece

**DETAIL:
ACCOUNTING FOR
THE OFFSET DISTANCE**

Offset distance

Template guide

Template guide will follow cutout in Masonite, but offset between edge of bit and outside of template guide's collar must be taken into consideration. That distance must be doubled because you're routing to both sides of the bit.

support the leaves. If they're too long, they'll lift the table and stress the hinges connecting the leaves to the table.

Each gate leg also needs to be tall enough to support its leaf without any sag. Leaves that are perfectly flush with the center portion of the tabletop are what you're looking for. The problem is that if your leg is at just the right height, there's virtually no clearance to swing the gate by the leaf without scraping the bottom of the leaf. To prevent this scarring, I cut the leg between 1/16 in. and 1/8 in. less than I really wanted it to be, and later I screwed a wedge in place on the underside of the table to make up for that shortfall (see the drawing on the facing page). This provides the necessary clearance and gives a nice, flat appearance across the whole top.

■ Table-Saw Tenoning Jig

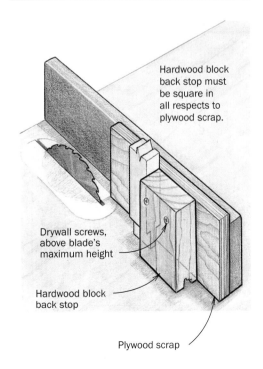

Hardwood block back stop must be square in all respects to plywood scrap.

Drywall screws, above blade's maximum height

Hardwood block back stop

Plywood scrap

I like low-tech solutions, and I'm not given to buying expensive jigs or fixtures when I can make my own. For the mortises on this table, I made a template-routing fixture for my plunge router. It consists of a little piece of Masonite nailed to a squared scrap of hardwood, and it takes less than a half-hour to lay out and build (see the top drawing on p. 111).

I use a piece of Masonite® wider than my workpiece and the scrap hardwood side by side to give my plunge router a stable platform. The hardwood scrap should be a little less deep than the workpiece, so the workpiece can be clamped to the bench. I figure out the distance from the inside edge of the hardwood scrap, which sets against the face of my workpiece, to the center of the workpiece and mark this distance on the underside of the Masonite.

I make the cutout in the Masonite as wide as my template guide. To get the correct mortise length, I add twice the offset distance (from the edge of my router bit to the outside of the template-guide collar) to the mortise length and mark that overall length on the underside of the Masonite (see the detail in the top drawing on p. 111).

To make the cutout in the Masonite, I set up the fence on my router table so that the bit is centered on what will be the center of the mortise cutout in the Masonite, and I rout away. I use the penciled marks on the underside of the Masonite as my stop marks. Because the hardwood block is squared, I can use it as a reference surface against my router table's fence.

SIMPLE AND ACCURATE MORTISING. The author's template-guide fixture makes for accurate mortises as long as they're laid out properly and the router is held square to the workpiece. He plunges and routs a little at a time to save wear on the router's bearings.

To rout the mortise, I simply clamp the fixture to my workpiece, clamp the workpiece to my bench, and have at it (see the photo above). The template guide takes care of the rest.

My table-saw tenoning jig is simpler yet. I take a length of plywood a bit shorter than my rip fence and glue and screw a 4- or 5-in.-high block of hardwood scrap to it so that the forward face of the block is at 90 degrees to the table (see the bottom drawing on p. 111). If you screw the block to the plywood as I did, make sure you do so above the maximum height of your table-saw blade. My right hand presses the workpiece and plywood tight against the rip fence. My left hand keeps the workpiece snug against the plywood and the hardwood block as I guide the workpiece through the blade (see the photo below). You could also attach a toggle clamp to the hardwood block to hold the workpiece in place for more safety.

I cut the shoulders of the tenons first, using a regular crosscut box, and then I rough-cut the cheeks on the bandsaw. I take the cheeks down to final thickness (dictated by my mortises) on the table saw with this simple jig.

FROM THE SCRAP BIN, A SERVICEABLE, DEPENDABLE TENONING JIG. It may not look like much, but the author's tenoning jig has seen more than a few projects go out of the shop over the years. An accurate 90-degree back stop is all it takes; careful guiding of the workpiece does the rest.

MAKING THE OVAL TABLETOP

The tabletop is an oval measuring 60 in. by 82 in. I laid out a quarter of an oval on some thick paper folded in quarters. I cut out the quarter-oval, unfolded the paper, and retraced the whole oval onto a sheet of cardboard to get some idea of how the tabletop would look. I used this rough pattern to lay up boards for the tabletop. If a board had a knot or defect at one end, I used it where that end would be cut off during the final shaping. I glued up my top and leaves, sanded them, cut and shaped the rule joints, and hinged the leaves to the center of the top, all before I cut my oval.

I roughed out the oval with a sabersaw, a good blade, and a steady hand. For the finish-cut, though, I created a router jig based on the instructions for drawing an ellipse in Ernest Joyce's *Encyclopedia of Furniture Making* (Sterling Publishing Co. Inc., 1987). I used my plunge router to make the cuts just ⅛ in. deep each pass. I took my time to minimize tearout, especially at the two sections where I was cutting against the grain. The final pass, which uses the entire cutting edge of the router bit, needs to be done very slowly and carefully. Once it's cut, though, you have a perfect oval that needs just a bit of sanding along its edge.

One other feature I added to the top is a pair of battens beneath each leaf to keep the leaves flat. I positioned them right behind the wedges, so they also prevent the gates from rotating too far. The center part of the tabletop extends far enough out to the sides that the top rail doesn't get in the way of the battens or prevent them from hanging straight down.

PAUL HARRELL

Using Shop-Sawn Veneer

I recently came upon a beautiful plank of jarrah—hard, heavy Australian wood—that was exactly what I wanted for a piece of furniture I was planning. The plank was small, though, only 5 ft. long, 1¾ in. thick, and less than 6 in. wide. The only way I could get much use out of it was to saw it into veneer. With some careful planning, I squeezed out of it all the veneers and edge-bandings I needed to make the sideboard shown in the photo on the facing page. The same plank, just about 4 bd. ft., wouldn't have been enough to make the top of the piece if I'd used it as solid.

I make my veneer on the bandsaw, as shown in the photo on p. 118, cutting sheets 3⁄32 in. thick, which is thick enough to be worked much like solid wood with both hand and power tools. It's also stiff enough to be edge-joined with wedge-clamp pressure. The finished surface is more forgiving and durable than thinner commercial veneer (generally, 1⁄28 in.). I also prefer shop-sawn veneer to the commercial variety because I can cut the solid-wood parts of a piece (legs, frame members, edge-bandings, pulls) from the same planks as the veneer. This means more control in matching grain and color patterns throughout the piece.

VENEER OR SOLID WOOD?

There are several reasons I might decide to use veneer instead of solid wood in a piece of furniture. Clean lines and the lack of end grain give veneered work a refinement that fits some pieces better than others. If I were making a table or a case piece for a formal dining room, for instance, I'd consider using veneer; in a kitchen table, where veneer seems out of place, I'd probably use solid wood. Because wood movement is not a problem with veneered panels, they offer options not available with solid wood. The top of the sideboard, for example, has a pattern involving cross-grain pieces and inlay that would quickly self-destruct in solid wood.

Veneer can add strength, too. A veneered back panel, glued in, gives rigidity to a case. Veneered tops can be solidly attached, and partitions and drawer runners can be glued into veneered carcases. All of this gives a strong and stable construction. For a detailed look at the ways I used veneer and solid wood, see the sidebars on pp. 117 and 120–121.

One thing veneering won't do is save time. Doing quality veneer work always takes longer than working with solid wood, and I do it only when the possibilities it offers really fit the piece.

SIDEBOARD SQUEEZED FROM A SMALL PLANK. By doing his own sawing, the author coaxed the primary veneer and edging for this sideboard from a single plank of jarrah. The legs, stretchers, and lighter veneer are mahogany.

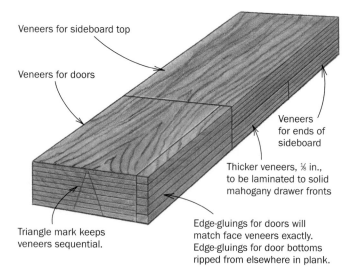

Veneers for sideboard top

Veneers for doors

Veneers for ends of sideboard

Thicker veneers, ⅛ in., to be laminated to solid mahogany drawer fronts

Triangle mark keeps veneers sequential.

Edge-gluings for doors will match face veneers exactly. Edge-gluings for door bottoms ripped from elsewhere in plank.

The author chose the more highly figured end of the plank for the door veneers. The pattern worked well vertically and would have been unbalanced if used on the top.

LAYING OUT A PLANK

Before making any cuts, I take time to look at the milled plank or planks and decide how the grain patterns will work best with the various parts of the piece I'm planning, as shown in the drawing above. I make sure there will be enough wood for all the veneers, plus pieces for edge-gluings and, in some cases, legs and stretchers. Both sides of every panel must be veneered to keep the stresses balanced, but for surfaces that won't show, I use veneer from less desirable parts of the plank or from a different wood.

After deciding how to use the plank, I cut it into manageable pieces before sawing the veneer. Sawing veneer from large, heavy planks is difficult and best avoided. I look for places to crosscut long pieces and usually rip wide planks before sawing the veneer. Even if I had a bandsaw with 10 in. or 12 in. under the guides, I wouldn't attempt to saw veneer that wide. Better results will come by ripping the plank in half, sawing veneers from the narrower

pieces, then edge-joining the veneers to restore the full width.

Although I do a lot of careful planning, I try to remain flexible. A thick plank may have defects inside that make some of the veneer unusable. Or, if I'm lucky, there may be some beautiful color or pattern I hadn't anticipated. After looking at all the veneer, I may make changes in some of the dimensions or even major changes in the design to make the best use of the wood.

SAWING VENEER

You don't need a large, expensive bandsaw to saw your own veneer, but you do need one that is well-tuned. Sharp blades are essential. Start with a new one, and change it when it starts to dull. The most obvious sign of dulling is increased resistance to feeding. But also keep an eye on the quality of the cut. A dull blade leaves a more ragged surface and may give a bowed rather than a perfectly vertical cut. Half-inch skip tooth blades with three or four teeth per inch are good resaw blades. Larger blades often have too much set and produce more sawdust and fewer veneers.

The rip fence that comes with most bandsaws is inadequate for sawing veneer. A shopmade fence tall enough to support the full width of the wood and stopped just past the blade to let the sawn wood move will give much better results (see the photo on p. 118). Because it's held in place by clamps, you can angle it to follow the lead of the bandsaw blade. Bandsaw blades rarely want to cut at exactly 90 degrees to the front of the table. To find the lead of the blade, draw a line parallel to one edge of a piece of scrap, and bandsaw freehand partway along the line. Then turn off the saw, and set a bevel gauge so that its handle is along the front edge of the bandsaw table and its blade is along the edge of the scrap, as shown in the drawing on p. 118. Use the bevel to set the veneer fence.

It is important to maintain constant pressure against the fence when cutting veneer. Use a smooth, steady feed rate from

I made the pattern on the top of my sideboard by joining the veneers before gluing them to the plywood core. I began by edge-gluing four narrow pieces of jarrah for the center section. I squared the ends of this section, using a crosscut box on the table saw. Then I lightly shot the ends with a sharp jointer plane to eliminate irregularities in the sawn surface. Next, I glued the end veneers of the mahogany frame to the center section. The joint is edge grain to end grain, so I used a gap-filling glue from Garrett Wade (161 Avenue of the Americas, New York, NY 10013; 800-221-2942) that has a high solids content and fills the end grain nicely. I glued on these end pieces ¹⁄₃₂ in. over long and flushed them to the jarrah afterward. Then I glued on the front and back veneers of the mahogany frame. All these glue-ups were done with wedges.

I glued the completed top pattern to the core in my press setup (see the drawing on p. 123), simultaneously gluing a sheet of mahogany to the underside of the core. As with all veneer glue-ups, I cut the veneer so that its width and length were fractionally less than the core stock. When this came out of the press, I trimmed and planed the edges and applied ⅛-in. mahogany edge-gluings, mitered at the front corners and butted at the back. I cut the miters on the table saw and did final fitting with a 45-degree block on my shooting board. I trimmed the edgings flush to the veneer with a pair of handplanes (see the photo below). If there is any chance of tearout in the face veneer, I finish with a scraper. With the edge-gluings on, I routed a ⅛-in. by ⅛-in. rabbet around the top edge and glued a jarrah edge bead into it. I ripped the bead on the bandsaw and glued it in with the bandsawn edge outward. I use masking tape as a clamp, starting alternate pieces from below (inward pressure) and above (downward pressure). And I don't spare the tape. When I'm finished, there isn't any wood showing around the edge.

FLUSH-TRIMMING EDGING IS A TWO-PLANE PROCEDURE. One is set for a coarse cut; the other is set for a fine cut. On edge-gluings applied before face veneers, the outside corners must be crisp for a good joint.

TO BANDSAW ³⁄₃₂-IN. VENEERS, clamp a high, half-length fence to the saw table, angled to accommodate the natural drift of the blade. Rip wide boards for better resawing; then edge-glue to rejoin the veneers.

Finding a Bandsaw Blade's Natural Cutting Angle

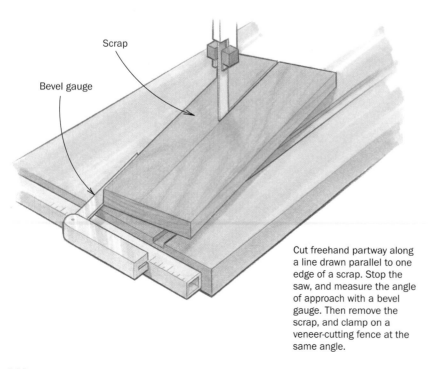

Scrap

Bevel gauge

Cut freehand partway along a line drawn parallel to one edge of a scrap. Stop the saw, and measure the angle of approach with a bevel gauge. Then remove the scrap, and clamp on a veneer-cutting fence at the same angle.

start to finish without stopping. I usually surface the plank with a light pass on the jointer between cuts. When the veneer is sawn, it should be stacked in the order it was cut and covered with a heavy piece of wood to keep it flat until you're ready to use it.

If the sawing goes well and the veneers are consistent in thickness, it is possible to glue them to the core as they come from the saw. I usually take one or two light passes through the planer, though, to ensure uniform thickness.

I have a small Inca jointer with a thicknessing attachment that works well cleaning up the veneers. Its lack of a power feed is an advantage when planing veneer. Large power-feed planers, especially those with segmented feed rollers, tend to eat veneer. Clamping a piece of plywood across the infeed and outfeed tables, covering up the bed rollers, may solve this dietary problem. You can use the same arrangement if your planer won't adjust low enough to plane veneer.

EDGE-JOINING VENEERS

The next step in preparing the veneer is edge-joining the pieces to get the widths I need. I lay out all the veneers, and then I make final decisions on how to use them, trying various patterns. I do this for all the surfaces at the same time so that I can see the effect of different arrangements. When I'm satisfied, I mark across the face of each group of veneers with a triangle to keep them in order. If there is any trimming to width or length to be done, I use the table saw just as I do with thicker stock.

Shoot the edges

I take a pair of veneers to be joined and, using a shooting board, shoot the edges with a sharp jointer plane, as shown in the photo at right. I do the shooting with one veneer faceup, the other facedown. This compensates for a plane that may not be cutting at exactly 90 degrees to the shooting board. Then I try the joint: It should be tight along its entire length with little pressure. Because veneers are somewhat flexible, it is possible to pull a badly fitting joint together, but don't be tempted. Take the time to shoot one or both edges again until the fit is right.

Wedge-glue the edge joints

The edge-joining goes quickly. With the veneers on a flat surface, I use pairs of wooden wedges to apply pressure, as shown in the photo below. Two strips of wood clamped to the benchtop are all you need for stops. They should be parallel, and about ½ in. farther apart than the width of the two veneers. I put a bead of glue on the edge of one veneer; then I put both veneers down between the wooden strips and push the joint together. A strip of newspaper keeps me from gluing to the benchtop. I use one hand to press down on the veneers at the joint while using the other to tighten the wedges. With all the wedges hand tight, I check the joint and then tap the wedges with a small hammer to set them. This technique makes it easy to keep the veneers flat during glue-up and also works well when gluing other thin stock, like drawer bottoms. Accurately jointed edges require minimal clamping pressure, which keeps the veneer from buckling.

CORE MATERIALS

I generally glue sawn veneer to a core of Baltic-birch plywood. It is readily available in a variety of thicknesses and is strong. Lumber core plywood also works well but, unfortunately, can rarely be found in anything but ¾-in. thickness in this country. Medium-density fiberboard (MDF) and sheet goods of this type might be suitable,

ERROR-FREE EDGE-JOINTING. Prepare veneers for edge-gluing by jointing them in pairs on the shooting board. Lay one veneer faceup and the other facedown to compensate for any error in the angle of the plane blade.

THICK VENEERS EDGE-GLUE LIKE SOLID WOOD. Lay the pieces to be joined between two fixed clamping boards. Hold the workpieces flat near the joint with one hand as you tighten a series of wedges with the other to apply pressure.

Veneered panels deliver a number of clear advantages over the traditional solid-wood frame and panel, which has to accommodate wood movement and relies solely on its frame for rigidity. The drawing illustrates the advantages of veneered panels in a variety of applications.

End panels, 1 in. thick, create a large gluing surface, free from wood movement, for a rock-solid end assembly. The construction can eliminate the need for stretchers.

Back panel, ⅜ in., is glued into a rabbet, providing racking resistance. Bottom panels are also glued in place.

Partitions: Because the partitions won't move with the seasons, the drawer-runner frames can be let into them and glued along their full length.

Doors: The stability of the plywood core is particularly welcome in an unfixed member like a door. Besides keeping the doors flat, the lack of seasonal movement permits fitting to much closer tolerances in the door opening.

Top: Because it won't move, the top can be joined solidly to the ends, stretchers, and partitions, increasing resistance to sagging. The stability also permits cross-grain patterning.

■ Building a Sideboard with Shop-Sawn Veneer

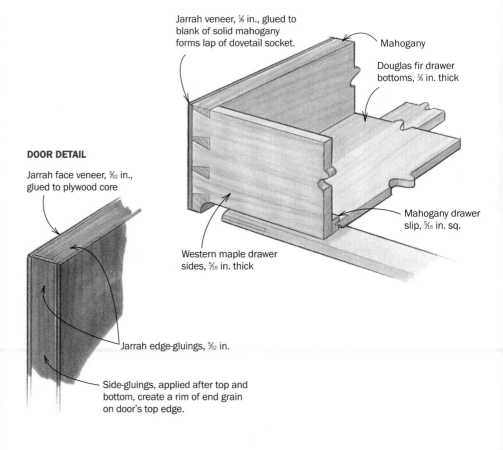

HALF-BLIND DOVETAILED DRAWER

Jarrah veneer, ⅛ in., glued to blank of solid mahogany forms lap of dovetail socket.

Mahogany

Douglas fir drawer bottoms, ¼ in. thick

Mahogany drawer slip, ⁵⁄₁₆ in. sq.

Western maple drawer sides, ⁵⁄₁₆ in. thick

DOOR DETAIL

Jarrah face veneer, ³⁄₃₂ in., glued to plywood core

Jarrah edge-gluings, ⁵⁄₃₂ in.

Side-gluings, applied after top and bottom, create a rim of end grain on door's top edge.

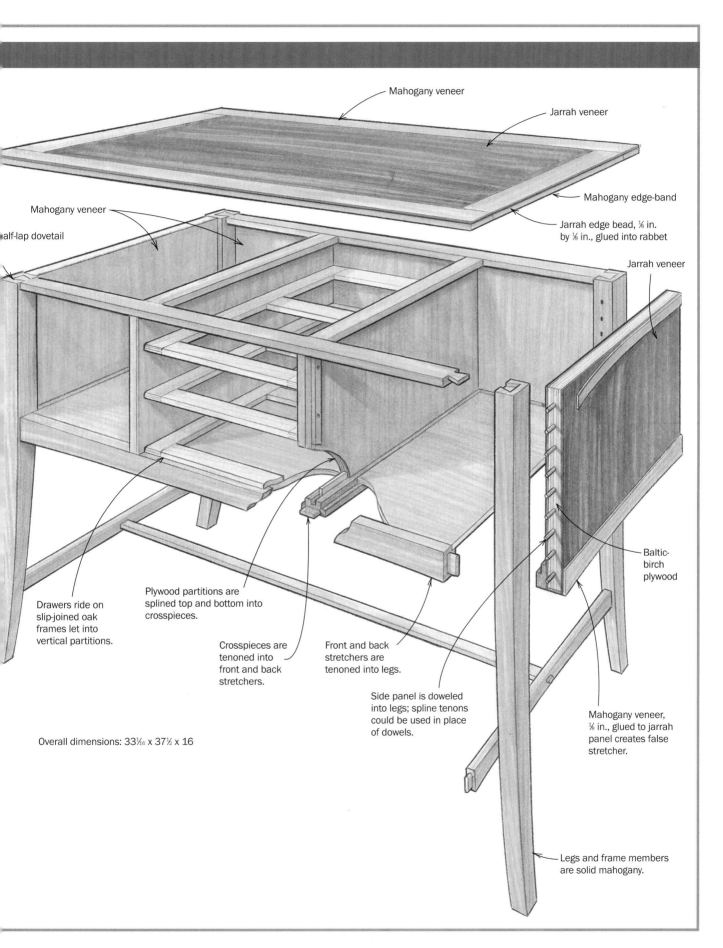

Mahogany veneer

Jarrah veneer

Mahogany veneer

Half-lap dovetail

Mahogany edge-band

Jarrah edge bead, ⅛ in. by ⅛ in., glued into rabbet

Jarrah veneer

Baltic-birch plywood

Drawers ride on slip-joined oak frames let into vertical partitions.

Plywood partitions are splined top and bottom into crosspieces.

Crosspieces are tenoned into front and back stretchers.

Front and back stretchers are tenoned into legs.

Side panel is doweled into legs; spline tenons could be used in place of dowels.

Mahogany veneer, ⅛ in., glued to jarrah panel creates false stretcher.

Legs and frame members are solid mahogany.

Overall dimensions: 33¹⁄₁₆ x 37½ x 16

Veneer, ³⁄₃₂ in., can be applied as an edge-gluing after face veneers (above) or before (below), which leaves faces uninterrupted.

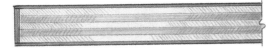

With larger edge-gluings, shapes can be worked on the edge with hand tools or a router.

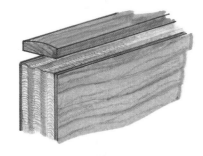

Even cleanly cut plywood edges show a washboard effect. For a tight joint, take down the end-grain bumps with a slightly convex scraper or a narrow sanding block before gluing on the edging. Be sure to avoid shaving the face veneers.

too, but I avoid them. I'm not convinced they're strong enough for some applications, and I don't like the smell and the dust they make in the shop. And MDF is terrible for planes and other hand tools. In some cases, when I need an unusual thickness, I'll make my own plywood core stock. I just stack an odd number of veneers with the grain in each sheet running at 90 degrees to its neighbors and glue them together in my veneer press.

It's important that your core stock be flat. Buy it flat, and store it so it stays flat. You can stack it horizontally or vertically, as long as it's fully supported. Lean it against a wall, and it's sure to warp. Some warpage can be flattened in the veneering process, but it's better not to count on it. Perfectly flat core stock is vital for surfaces that will be unsupported, like cabinet doors or desk fall flaps.

PREPARE FOR THE PRESS

With all the veneers edge-joined and the plywood cut to size, I get ready to glue up. If any of the plywood is going to get edge-gluings before veneering, I do that next. (For a range of options in edging veneered panels, see the drawing at left.)

I use a cabinet scraper to clean up the glue squeeze-out at joints in the veneer. Then I give both sides of the plywood and the bottom surface of the veneers a quick rub with 280-grit sandpaper: An oxidized surface is no good for gluing. Neither is a dusty one, so I clean off the sanded surfaces with the brush attachment on my shop vacuum and wipe them down with a clean cloth. Finally, it's a good idea to mark the veneers and core clearly, so a veneer doesn't get turned the wrong way during the glue-up.

I use yellow glue for most veneering. For something that will take a long time to clamp up (a large tabletop or a curved door), plastic resin glue will give a longer open time. I spread the glue with a scrap of veneer that has an edge notched on the bandsaw. (The kerfs are about ⅛ in. deep, and the teeth between them are the same width as the kerfs, 1⁄16 in. or so.) Working quickly, I spread the glue evenly on one side of the plywood and then place the veneer on the glued surface. I turn the whole thing over, glue the other side of the plywood and apply the veneer to that side. To keep the veneers from shifting in the press, I hammer a few small brads into what will become waste at each end. If there is no extra length that can be cut off after the glue-up, I use masking tape to hold everything in place. I start a piece of tape on the face of one veneer, pull it down tightly over the edge of the core, and onto the other veneer. Three or four pieces along each side of the panel should keep things from shifting.

INTO THE VENEER PRESS

The basic clamp-and-caul veneer press, shown in the drawing above, is probably the simplest and least expensive setup for pressing veneers, but there are many possibilities. Veneer screws in frames are powerful, if bulky. A vacuum press, if you do enough veneering to justify the cost, is ideal. It equalizes the pressure perfectly over the entire surface of the veneer and can be used to do curved as well as flat surfaces. If you use a setup like mine, tighten the clamps in the center of the panel first, and move outward toward the edges. This avoids trapping glue in the center of the panel.

I usually leave a panel in the press for at least four hours. When it comes out of the press, the glue will have set, but the panel will still contain a lot of moisture from the glue. Never let a freshly veneered panel dry faster on one side than the other, or it will

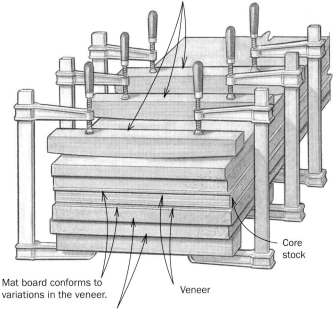

Softwood cauls, crowned about 1⁄16 in. along the bottom edge, contact the middle first and distribute pressure across the glue-up.

Core stock

Mat board conforms to variations in the veneer.

Veneer

Layers of ¾-in. MDF spread the clamping pressure and ensure a flat panel.

Veneer is held in register during glue-up with brads or tape.

cup. When a panel comes out of the press, I stand it on end, so it is exposed to the air on both sides. Another alternative is to put it flat on the bench, cover it with a piece of plywood or MDF, and weight it down. Once a panel dries completely (in one or two days), it will be stable.

When the panel is dry, I straighten and square one edge on the jointer. I trim the other three sides on the table saw to within 1⁄32 in. or so of final dimension and clean up the edges with a jointer plane. Then I'm ready to apply the edge-gluings or cut the joints.

DARRYL KEIL

Strategies for Curved Work

The traditional method of making curved, laminated parts such as doors or aprons requires male and female forms and a barrel of clamps to squeeze the layers into shape. Or you can use a single form and a vacuum press, essentially a sealed plastic bag connected to a vacuum pump. A vacuum press speeds up production, does away with cumbersome clamps, and reduces the amount of material needed for forms.

Although I've done it a thousand times or more, every time I fire up my vacuum press and see the bag shrink itself around a project, contorting wood into a new shape, I'm awed by the power of Mother Nature.

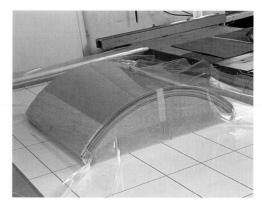

IN THE BAG. A vacuum press simplifies the job of building forms and clamping curved parts during glue-up.

Atmospheric pressure, when properly harnessed, can generate more force than any other tool in my shop.

On average, an object in a vacuum bag experiences about 12 psi, which really doesn't sound like much. But the numbers quickly add up as an object gets larger. For example, I made a form for laminated credenza doors measuring 24 in. by 27 in. The vacuum press delivered a cumulative pressure of 7,776 lb., almost 4 tons, over this form. I couldn't duplicate that kind of clamping force even if I parked my tractor on top of a glue-up.

As a manufacturer of vacuum-press systems, I get a lot of calls from people who run into difficulties with the process. Over the years I've developed a number of methods that help ensure good results. These include building strong forms, choosing the proper core materials and glues, and preparing veneers for trouble-free bonding. Whether you use one of a number of commercially made systems or build your own vacuum press, these techniques apply.

MAKE FORMS RIGID IN THE RIGHT PLACES

The shotgunlike blast of a form imploding under full vacuum presents a powerful lesson in how not to build a form. But getting it right isn't always so obvious.

I make forms using plywood, particleboard, and bending plywood. Convex forms are the most common ones used in vacuum veneering. With a convex form you can make doors, table aprons, even half columns. A vacuum bag works best around a convex form.

Concave forms present special problems because the vacuum bag tends to lock at the high points, bridging over concave sections. If a project does call for a form with a concave section, press the concave section into place before turning on the press. I tell people just to climb up on the bag and stand on the form, then turn on the press.

Design the piece first, then dimension the form

Accurate, detailed drawings are a must when working with curves. From these drawings you can figure out the dimensions of a form. When working with curved parts, the radii of the inside and outside faces of parts are different. That's also true of a form (see the drawing below). Make the form about 1 in. longer and wider than the final dimension to allow for trimming the glued-up pieces.

A form consists of a base, interior ribs, and blocking, and a layer or two of "skin." If the ribs are spaced too far apart or there isn't enough skin strength, a form will distort and possibly implode. A distorted form will distort a glued-up part. Distortion may also result in poor pressing, which results in poor adhesion between laminations.

The base is a sheet of ¼-in. to ¾-in. plywood or particleboard (the thickness is not that critical). Ribs are ¾-in. plywood or particleboard (see the photo on p. 126). Ribs should be placed 3 in. o.c. when using one layer of skin; 6 in. o.c. when making a double skin.

■ Sizing Parts for Typical Forms and Cores

When calculating the radius of the ribs, remember to subtract the thicknesses of the finished stock plus the skin of the form to get the correct arc.

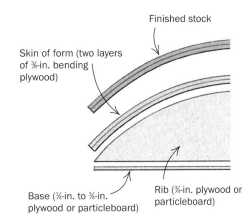

Finished stock

Skin of form (two layers of ⅜-in. bending plywood)

Base (¼-in. to ¾-in. plywood or particleboard)

Rib (¾-in. plywood or particleboard)

The skin is made of one or two layers of ¾-in. bending plywood. This material bends only one way and remains fairly stiff in the other direction. Avoid using ⅛-in. bending plywood for forms because three layers of it do not equal the strength of one layer of ¾-in. material. Each layer of ⅛-in. plywood will flex independently under pressure and produce a wavy form.

Cut the base first and make sure the corners are square. Then cut the ribs and nail them to the base. The ribs on the ends of the form require additional bracing because the force of the vacuum places equal pressure on all sides of the form. Place vertical cross braces between the outside ribs and their neighbors, approximately 10 in. o.c.

■ Making a Sturdy Form

A GOOD RIB JOINT. Forms must withstand great forces. Use ¾-in. particleboard or plywood for ribs. Place them 6 in. o.c., and add blocking to the ends.

Nail or screw the skin onto the ribs (see the top photo below). When nailing, apply a bead of glue to the two outside ribs so the nails alone do not bear the inward pressure. If using screws, countersink them and fill the depressions with putty.

Last, cut a slot in the underside of the form by running it across the table saw. Raise the blade just high enough to cut all

the way through the bottom of the form (see the bottom photo). The slot will allow air to escape from the inside of the form when a vacuum is drawn.

PREPARE THE CORE

I build most curved parts in two steps. First I lay up the core. (For more on core materials, see the sidebar on p. 130.) Once that cures, I apply the veneer. Trying to do it all at once can be a frantic undertaking. Because I do it in two steps, I don't waste veneer if something goes wrong with the core.

Cut the core stock, leaving an extra ¾ in. all around for trimming. Make the top piece of bending plywood a little wider because it will have a slightly larger radius. To help stiffen the core, sandwich a sheet of backer-grade veneer between the plywood (see the drawing on p. 128). Orient the veneer cross-grain to the plywood. To keep parts lined up, draw a centerline down the apex of the form and mark the center of the core plies.

After applying glue to the core parts, place them on the form. Apply tape to keep parts from shifting (see the top photo on p. 128). Mark both the form and the core again to remind yourself which way the core was placed on the form. (Later, when gluing on the veneer, return the core to the same spot on the form for a good fit.) Place everything in the bag and run the vacuum.

Wood and wood products don't always come out of a glue-up exactly the way you want them. There's usually a small amount of springback. It's impossible to calculate how much; let experience be your guide. When laminating ⅜-in. bending plywood, don't be overly concerned if the part comes out of the press and suffers what seems like excessive springback. Once you add the two-ply face veneers, it will likely hold its shape. On the other hand, laminated ⅛-in. ply-

SKIN DEEP. Nail or screw two layers of ⅜-in. bending plywood over the ribs. Make the form slightly larger than the workpiece's final dimensions to allow for trimming.

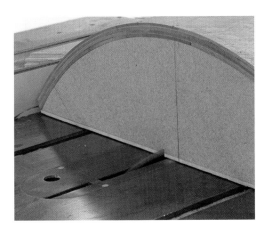

CUT A SLOT ON THE UNDERSIDE OF THE FORM. The slot allows air to be evacuated from inside the form when it is under vacuum.

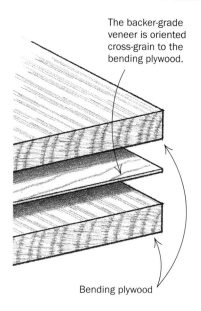

The backer-grade veneer is oriented cross-grain to the bending plywood.

Bending plywood

TAPE THE CORE LAYERS ONTO THE FORM BEFORE PUTTING THEM INTO THE VACUUM-PRESS BAG. A typical core consists of two layers of ⅜-in. bending plywood with a sheet of backer-grade veneer sandwiched (cross-grain) in between.

SOURCES OF SUPPLY

Berkshire Veneer Co.
29 Locust Hill Rd., Great Barrington, MA 01230; 877-836-3379

Certainly Wood
13000 Route 78, E. Aurora, NY 14052; 716-655-0206

Constantine's
2050 Eastchester Rd., Bronx, NY 10461; 800-223-8087

Flamingo Veneer Co.
356 Glenwood Ave., E. Orange, NJ 07017; 973-672-7600

Flexible Materials
11209 Electron Dr., Louisville, KY 40299; 502-267-7717

Mercury Vacuum Presses
PO Box 2232, Fort Bragg, CA 95437; 800-995-4506 or 707-964-7557

Quality VAKuum Products
43 Bradford St., Concord, MA 01742; 800-547-5484

Vacuum Pressing Systems
553 River Rd., Brunswick, ME 04011; 207-725-0935

HELP THE VACUUM BAG DO ITS JOB. Press the core down as the bag draws a vacuum.

wood tends to hold its shape better because of the extra plies.

GLUE TWO-PLY VENEERS ONTO THE CORE

I call two-ply veneer, or two-ply, curved-panel insurance. It's an extra step, but one that protects your project. Two-ply consists of a face veneer and a backer-grade veneer, such as mahogany, glued cross-grain to one another (see the drawing on p. 130). I sandwich two-plies between hardboard and glue them up using the vacuum press (see the photo below). Two-plies are also available commercially.

There are many good reasons for using two-plies: (1) problems in the face veneer, such as bubbling or wrinkling, can be repaired from the back side before gluing the veneer onto the core; (2) the ⅜-in. bending plywood has a rough texture, and a single sheet of veneer glued over it may telegraph that texture (two-ply won't); (3) when gluing the two-ply to the core, minor areas of poor adhesion will be bridged by the two-ply and will not wrinkle or bubble; and (4) two-ply is stiff enough to be taped to a workbench and sanded while it's still flat. Sanding curved surfaces, especially concave areas, is difficult.

When veneering, treat both faces of the core the same way. If you glue a two-ply to the face of the core, glue a two-ply to the back as well; otherwise, the project will warp. Glue both the face and back two-plies to the core in one pressing. Spread the glue on the core, not on the veneer, which would curl. Then place the back two-ply on the form, place the core over it, and the face two-ply on top. Tape the top edge to the form to keep it from slipping, and place the assembly in the bag. No cover sheets are required.

ONCE THE CORE HAS CURED, GLUE ON THE INNER AND OUTER SKINS OF VENEER. The author uses two-ply on both the front and back. Two-plies help eliminate problems such as wrinkling and bubbling. Also, they can be sanded before glue-up.

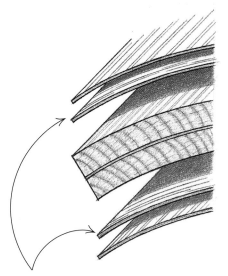

Two layers of veneer (two-ply) glued cross-grain to each other are used on both faces of the core.

CORE MATERIALS FOR CURVED WORK

In curved veneer work, I use bending plywoods for the substrate or core. The most commonly used cores are ⅛-in. Italian poplar plywood (A) and ¼-in. or ⅜-in. lauan bending plywood (B)— a common brand is called Wigglewood®.

These plywoods may be ordered with long grain, called 4-by-8 (makes an 8-ft.-long tube), or cross-grain, called 8-by-4 (makes a 4-ft.-long tube). The ⅛-in. plywood can be bent into a tighter radius than the ⅜-in. plywood, and it also has a smoother surface.

If a project requires parts that are light in weight, you may want to consider thick, resin-impregnated kraft-paper honey-

comb (C) for the core material. The honeycomb must be sheathed with ⅛-in. bending plywood and edge-banded with either plywood or solid stock.

TRIM THE FINISHED PIECE, USING THE FORM AS A GUIDE

Once the face veneers have been glued onto the core, the piece must be trimmed square before edge-banding can be applied. In the case of a typical glue-up, such as a door, there are four edges to trim. To get the first reference edge, clamp the piece to the form, leaving a slight overhang, and trim one end using a router and a flush-trimming bit. Simply let the bit's bearing ride along the edge of the form (see the top photo on the facing page).

It's next to impossible to keep a router from tipping slightly while moving along a curve, but don't worry if the cut has a few minor dips. Next, trim the opposite side on the table saw, using either the rip fence or a crosscut sled (see the center photo on the facing page). Then flip the workpiece and make a final pass on the router-cut side.

The other two sides are ripped on the table saw, using the form as a sled (see the bottom photo on the facing page). Depending on the shape of the form, it may be necessary both to tip the form and to tilt the sawblade. Nail a strip of wood to the underside of the form to get the proper lift. Check the angle and make a trial cut, proud of the line. Make adjustments, if necessary. Cut the other side by flipping the workpiece around on the form.

Edge-banding goes on last

Although I don't like to use yellow glue for bent parts, it's perfect for edge-banding. Where possible, I clamp edge-banding in place (see the bottom photo on p. 133). But some parts can be difficult to clamp. In such cases, apply glue to the edge of the lamination and the edge-banding, let it set for about an hour, then attach the edge-

Trimming the Workpiece

TRIM ONE END OF THE WORKPIECE, USING THE FORM AS A GUIDE. The author uses a router with a long, flush-trimming bit.

CUT THE OTHER END PARALLEL TO THE FIRST. Masking tape applied to the veneer helps prevent tearout. Crosscut the router-trimmed side again, if necessary, using the table saw.

USE THE FORM AS A SLED FOR MAKING RIP CUTS. To get the proper angle, a strip of wood has been tacked to the base of the form. Make the first cut proud of the line and check the angle. Tilt the blade as necessary.

U rea resin glue is ideal for veneering, especially when working with curved forms. Urea resin comes in two forms, a liquid resin that is mixed with a powdered catalyst and a powder that mixes with water. Both types of glue are easy to work, have long open times, and become very rigid when cured. Rigidity translates into less springback.

Epoxy and polyurethane glues may also be used, although they are more difficult to apply because of their thick viscosity. Both also produce more bleed-through. The first time you have to sand and scrape epoxy off veneer will probably be your last.

White and yellow polyvinyl acetate (PVA) glues don't dry as rigid as the aforementioned glues and have short open times, making them a poor choice for curved work. Contact cement is also a poor choice because it remains flexible when cured.

A FOAM ROLLER SPREADS GLUE EVENLY. The author prefers two-part urea resin glues for curved work because the glue, once cured, is very rigid.

HOW MUCH GLUE IS RIGHT? A finger swiped across the glued surface should produce a shallow ridge.

EDGE-BANDING CAN ALSO BE IRONED IN PLACE. Coat the edges of the core and veneer with yellow glue and let them set for an hour before ironing.

banding using a household iron (see the photo above). The heat reactivates the glue. Immediately after ironing, rub the edge-banding with a block of wood to help seat the veneer.

For your first curved project, start with something small, like a curved drawer front or the top of a jewelry box. Once you feel confident with curved-panel components, you may have a hard time not including them in your work. Curves bring life to furniture. A piece with sinuous lines seems poised to go somewhere. With the addition of highly figured veneers, it's poised to go somewhere in high style.

CLAMP EDGE-BANDING VENEER ONTO THE ENDS OF THE WORKPIECE. The author clamps directly to his workbench.

 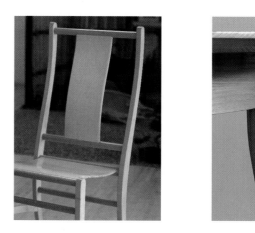 

Inspiration

Your work is a creative outlet. Sometimes you want to make a quick, simple project, sometimes you want to challenge yourself with an elaborate piece, and sometimes you're just not sure what you're looking for. That's where this section comes in. You'll find a variety of examples here to inspire you, and the specifications and design information will help you make the leap from inspiration to reality.

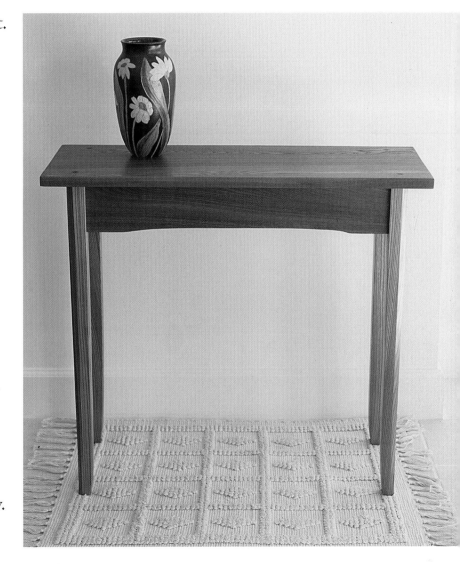

GENE MARTIN

Dining Set in Cherry and Imbuya

CHAIRS REFLECT TABLE DETAILS. After using imbuya for the contrasting inlays on the table, the author decided to make the chairs entirely of imbuya.

FINDING THE CORRECT CURVE. The author made a pine prototype of these chairs to make sure they would feel comfortable.

INLAYS EMBELLISHED WITH BRASS. It's hard to notice at first glance, but the imbuya inlays converge on the outside corners of the table legs. Where they meet, just a few inches above the floor, the author inlaid a diamond-shaped piece of brass.

Slender simplicity was the goal in designing this straightforward dining-room furniture. I didn't want to clutter the elegance of the design, so I used embellishments sparingly.

The table is cherry, which I chose for its durability and its warm, soft color. The inlays along the apron and down the legs are Brazilian imbuya. This dark wood accentuates the thin lines of the legs. It has a similar effect on the apron, drawing attention to the cove without overwhelming it.

Imbuya seemed like a natural selection for the chairs, providing contrast with the cherry and continuity with the inlay. After some sketches and a few conversations with the couple buying these pieces, I made a pine prototype. The prototype allowed the three of us to work out the angles and the height of the seat for a comfortable fit.

The final step in designing the chairs was to trim unnecessary bulk from the prototype without sacrificing strength. Paring down the back slats, the crest rail, and the legs reinforced the chair's slender lines.

SPECIFICATIONS

■ DIMENSIONS
Chairs: 18 in. wide, 20 in. deep, and 43 in. high

Table: 64 in. long, 44 in. wide and 30 in. high (80 in. with removable leaf)

■ MATERIALS
Cherry, imbuya, leather, and brass

■ FINISH
Oil

DARRELL PEART

Audio Cabinet in Cherry and Wenge

I proudly displayed my stereo gear on cinder blocks and pine planks when I was 18. As my woodworking skills improved, I built a monstrosity of a cabinet—it was the center of attention in my living room. Through its glass doors you could see all the meters, knobs, and switches that go along with electronic components.

When I designed this stereo cabinet, I wanted to hide the electronic gadgetry. I had in mind a less conspicuous piece,

something that would blend with the rest of my furniture, which is in the Arts and Crafts vein. I find the early-20th-century style simple and honest. I am fascinated by the use of exposed joinery as an integral part of the design.

This cabinet also displays the influence of contemporary furniture maker James Krenov. The rectangular cabinet, with the doors set inside the top and bottom case pieces and a separate leg structure to support the cabinet, is certainly a Krenov touch. The exposed joinery is common both to Krenov and to the Arts and Crafts designers. The rails connecting the legs have a detail suggestive of the "cloud-lift" motif employed by Arts and Crafts designers Charles and Henry Greene.

With the exception of the drawer bottoms, the piece is made entirely of solid

VISIBLE JOINERY. Exposed tenons, highlighted with wedges of padauk (base) and wenge (upper cabinet), draw attention to the joinery.

SPECIFICATIONS

■ DIMENSIONS
22 in. wide (at base), 48¾ in. high, and 18⅜ in. deep

■ MATERIALS
Cherry, wenge, and padauk

■ FINISH
Daly's ProFin oil

GADGETRY IS HIDDEN. The simple lines of this cabinet are influenced by the contemporary furniture maker James Krenov.

BASE DESIGN SEPARATES COMPONENTS. The half-lapped structure doweled to the frame of the base makes the cabinet appear to float above the legs.

wood. The case is cherry with wenge pulls and tenon wedges. The base is wenge with padauk tenon wedges. The top is located on the base with four dowels, and the two parts can be taken apart easily.

The case and the drawers are dovetailed. The frame-and-panel doors and the crisscross section of the base are half-lapped. The remaining joinery is mortise and tenon. One of the drawers is sized for cassettes, the other for compact discs, and the back has a removable panel to provide easy access to the electronics.

■ Base Construction

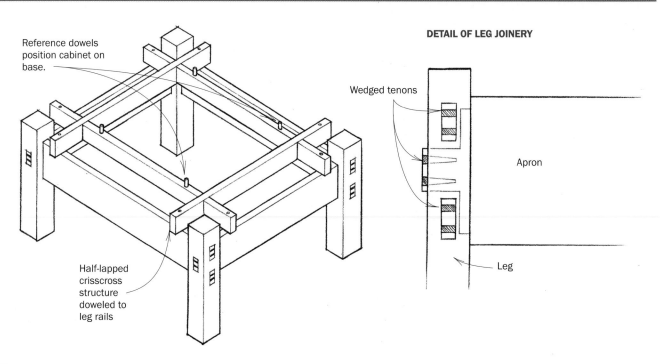

Reference dowels position cabinet on base.

Half-lapped crisscross structure doweled to leg rails

DETAIL OF LEG JOINERY

Wedged tenons

Apron

Leg

LOTS OF STORAGE AND AN EASY-ACCESS BACK. The removable back panel includes vent slits and a round cutout for wires. The two drawers are sized for cassettes and compact discs.

CHARLES E. JOHNSON

Lacewood Writing Desk

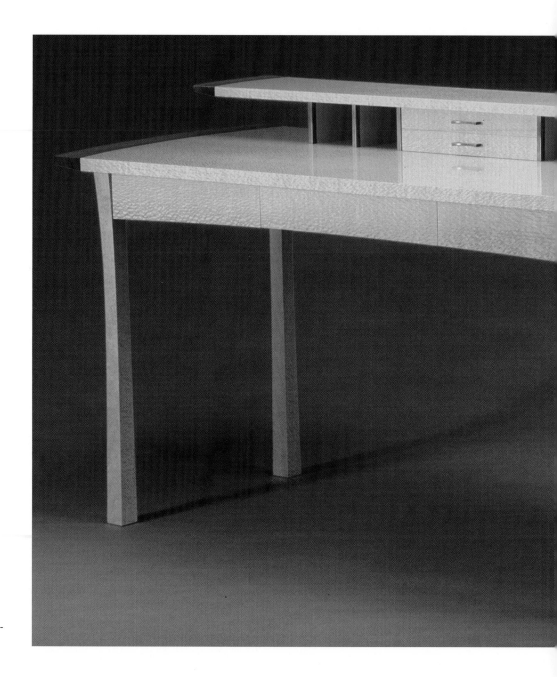

ARCHITECTURAL TRAINING SHADES DESIGN. Echoing houses designed by Frank Lloyd Wright, this desk has wide overhangs and a rectangular feel.

EXOTIC WOODS OFFER A CONTRAST. The only ornamentation on this writing desk is the contrast between the Australian lacewood and cocobolo accents.

This writing desk was commissioned by a client whose only requirements were that it be unique, functional, and visually compatible with the furniture she already owned.

I wanted a design with clean lines and a classic form. My sketches reminded me of some early Frank Lloyd Wright houses with long roof overhangs. The desk evolved into long rectangular shapes, although I used very delicate radii to soften the edges of the top, the legs, and the apron. I kept the piece completely free of any mechanical hardware.

I selected the wood after completing the final sketches, choosing unusual materials that would contrast with each other. The top is veneer over high-strength Baltic birch plywood. The other parts are of solid wood. I refined the design during construction, partially in response to advice from fellow craftsmen.

SPECIFICATIONS

■ DIMENSIONS
29 in. wide, 63 in. long, and 29 in. high

■ MATERIALS
Australian lacewood (veneer and solid wood), cocobolo drawer pulls and detailing, and maple drawer sides and runners

■ FINISH
Urethane-based nitrocellulose lacquer

GARY ROGOWSKI

Cloud Rise Bed

AN IMAGE FIT FOR SLUMBER. The cloud rise form, seen in the gently stepped rails of the headboard, adds lift to the strong horizontal lines.

loating clouds rising in the sky. Mist in the hills. What better form than the cloud rise to shape a bed? What better image for sleeping? Used by the Chinese for centuries in their furniture, the cloud rise gave me just the subtle accent I wanted for this bed. No blustery posts or gilded cherubs staring down at my sleeping customers; just a refined form with a few details was enough to satisfy my design sense and their taste.

This design, as with all others ever dreamed of in sleep or while awake, springs from several sources. The taper of the legs, flaring like trees as they descend to the ground, is a basic architectural form. Charles Rennie Mackintosh used it successfully in some of his furniture designs, and I liked the way it gave a solid and stable look to the bed posts. This became one of my starting forms.

Another dominant form—the overhanging rail in the headboard—is a feature I have always enjoyed in Chinese furniture. This same shape also can be found in Japanese temple design, particularly in the gates that front those sacred spaces. I felt the strong horizontal line contrasted nicely with the taper of the legs. It also seemed to fit well with the broad expanse of a futon or mattress that would fill the bed.

With my horizontals in place and the leg shape defined, I now had a frame within which to design some pleasing shapes. The cloud rise (also called a "cloud lift" in Greene and Greene furniture) became a focal point for both positive and negative shapes. I could use it in the headboard and footboard, creating shapes that would also define the negative space between these rails. In other words, the positive cloud rise in the headboard and footboard gives the negative spaces the same shape. I also used the cloud rise in the long bed rails in two versions of this design, and left them square in

ASIAN INSPIRATION. The cloud rise, seen here in the footboard, is a common feature in traditional Chinese furniture.

SPECIFICATIONS

■ DIMENSIONS
84 in. long, 66 in. wide, and 36 in. high

■ MATERIALS
Cherry and rosewood

■ FINISH
Oil and varnish mixture

a third version with a slightly different headboard (see the photos below).

A beautiful feature of a design like this is the freedom it allows when filling up the space within the structural frame of the headboard. There were, I discovered, many ways to divide and decorate this space. In the first rendition, I used tapered columns in both the footboard and headboard, simi-lar in shape to the bed legs, to help support the long top rails. Then I decided that a strong contrasting shape—a rosewood orb—would be a wonderful counterpoint to all those horizontal lines. In another version, I used three narrow horizontals, and in a third I decorated the headboard with two stylized seed forms, as shown in the photos below.

HEADBOARD IS A CANVAS.
The open-framed headboard can be divided and decorated in different ways. In this one, the central field is no longer solid, and the orb is larger.

SIMILAR DESIGN, DIFFERENT DETAILS. This variation on the cloud rise bed stresses the horizontal. The central image, a stylized seed pattern in rose-wood, provides contrast.

MICHAEL HURWITZ

Fresh Curves for a Kitchen Table

I've found that seemingly attractive commissions sometimes bring with them limitations that prove too restricting. But this project was an example of the ideal commission. The clients, who wanted a kitchen table for daily use, had seen two tables of mine that they liked—a decorative table with a marble mosaic top and a tea table with a slatted top. They liked the size and circular format of the center table, but were afraid that the marble top might be too cold or hard for a kitchen table. And the table's base didn't provide the necessary legroom for dining. They also liked the idea of activating the top surface by building it up of crisscrossing slats as I had done

SPECIFICATIONS

■ DIMENSIONS
Table: 42 in. in diameter and 30 in. high
Chairs: 17 in. wide, 18 in. deep, and
30½ in. high

■ MATERIALS
Table: Elm with elm and walnut veneer
Chairs: Ash

■ FINISH
Table: Oil and varnish
Chairs: Lacquered with milk paint on
the seats

BENDING BOTANICAL FORMS TO HUMAN USE. The high-hooping stretchers, inspired by plant forms, rise and cross creating footroom underneath.

SLATS WITHOUT SLOTS. Crisscrossing strips of walnut and elm veneer answer the customer's request for something that recalled Hurwitz's slat-topped tables but was fit for dining.

with the tea table, but they were concerned that it was less practical than a solid top would be.

I settled fairly quickly on a veneered pattern that would make a reference to the slatted solutions of previous pieces but would make a solid surface. As I designed the veneer pattern, I had in mind the way a woven tablecloth looks. I made a pattern that was simpler where it would be a backdrop for the place settings and slightly more complex in the center. I thought of it as a piece of fabric whose borders were unraveled, leaving only the woven center still intact.

In the base of the table I was taking cues from natural forms but tried to stylize them to the point where they're not really recognizable as sprouts or limbs, but still retain the feeling of something organic. The stretchers are plainly practical and structural—their hooped design provides knee room while keeping the table's legs from wiggling. But they also do visual work; they reinforce the sense of upward movement within the piece.

EACH LEG OF THE TABLE HAS A MATING TRUSS, WHICH FORKS AT THE TOP LIKE A TREE BRANCH. The trusses support the tabletop's rim and make a visual connection between the top and base.

WHEN THE CHAIRS ARE PUSHED IN, THEIR FRONT LEGS, which are turned out 45 degrees, nestle against the stretchers.

GARY NAKAMOTO

A Bent-Plywood Chair Built for Good Posture

SAWN CURVES AND BENT PLYWOOD AND CYLINDERS come together in this side chair to produce a gracefully curved shape. The same bending form was used to create the seat and the back.

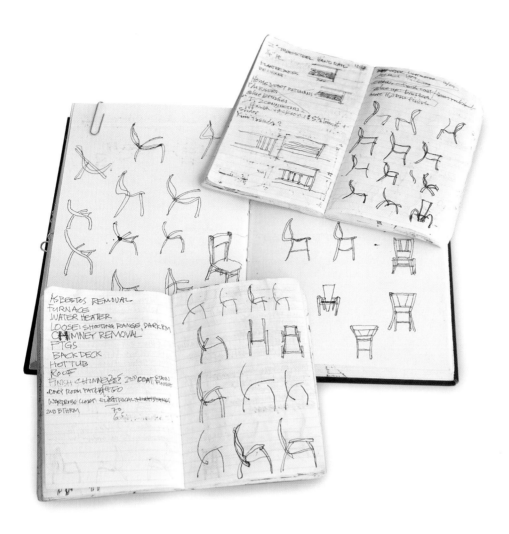

SKETCHING NEVER STOPS. As a student at the California College of Arts and Crafts, the author made numerous thumbnail sketches of chairs before developing one into a prototype. Even after three versions, he continues to play with the design.

I designed the prototype for these chairs while I was studying art at the California College of Arts and Crafts. My aim was to harmonize cylindrical elements with rectangular, the straight and angular with the curved and fluid. I wanted to balance structural soundness with light weight, elegance with straightforward joinery and, most importantly, good posture with comfort.

In the chairmaking class that I was taking, two San Francisco furniture makers—Carolyn and John Grew-Sheridan—demonstrated a bending form that produced a curved, laminated plywood seat. The intent of the form was to visually streamline the seat's profile by minimizing its thickness. The Grew-Sheridans graciously let me borrow the

SPECIFICATIONS

■ DIMENSIONS

19 in. wide, 22 in. deep, and 39 in. high

■ MATERIALS

Maple, red oak dowels, and birch plywood

AN ANGULAR VARIATION. After making the chair with curved legs and stretchers, the author decided to straighten out the parts, bringing down the cost of the chair and changing its look.

bending form, which I used to make several seats. As I played with them and tested them on other people in the class, I discovered that I could flip the seat over and use the same shape for the back of the chair.

The first version of this design (not shown here) was rather blocky and ponderous, although its construction was similar to that of the later versions. The plywood seat and back—made of three layers of $\frac{5}{32}$-inch birch plywood—are glued into grooves, or dadoes, in the cylindrical crest rail and seat rails. The cylinders have turned tenons at both ends that are glued into the legs.

I tried to refine the first version by adding curves to the legs and stretchers. I liked the play between the opposing curves

of the plywood and the legs and stretchers, but it made the construction much more complicated. With the final version, I returned to the rectilinear legs and stretchers, which speeds production considerably (see the photo above).

Throughout the evolution of these chairs the focus was on the comfort of the seat and the back. The curves and tilt of the seat allow the sitter to slide back into the chair while the curves of the back provide lumbar support and encourage good posture. I call the design the "G.S. Poschair" in an attempt to incorporate "posture" with "chair" while acknowledging the Grew-Sheridans' contribution.

PHILIP PONVERT

Circles, Inlays, and Curves Unite a Bedroom Suite

A SUITE OF COMMON ELEMENTS. Curves, contrast, and circles make all the furniture of this bedroom similar but not the same.

There is a list written on a piece of maple that hangs on my shop wall—four brief reminders that have kept me going on this room commission and others. "Keep Working," first on the list, is my best bet when I'm stuck in a design bind or just tired and confused. "Keep Smiling" is next; sometimes it can make a big difference.

"Always Improve" is true with all aspects of life but, in this case, it refers to my eye and my skills. Finally, "Be Smart with Money" is important to remember because frugality has been critical to my survival. I never want to hear someone say, "Oh, how nice, you used to make furniture?"

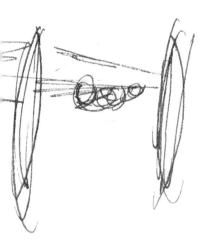

Through a series of rough sketches, the author eventually decided to use disks just to deflect the curved parts of the headboard and footboard, as shown in the bottom drawing.

This bedroom set is made primarily of 30-year-old walnut, cut and air-dried by an older gentleman in Ohio who has shown me much about wood. It was originally to be made of red oak and wenge, but plans change. Remember, "Keep Smiling."

The chest of drawers was the first piece I designed. The customers were intrigued by a smaller version I had made and wanted something with similar features, especially the unusual leg shape. Bringing the legs through the top of the bureau makes it quite different from other case pieces in which the top acts as a roof, capping all the vertical elements. I think this leg design allows the mirror to become more connected to the chest even though it hangs on the wall above it.

I don't like bombarding a customer with the same elements in each piece of furniture, especially those that share a room. The bed design, in this case, flowed from the mirror but did not copy it. Instead, we explored the use of the disks to "push" or "hold" the bent parts (although they don't actually do this; the curved pieces are steam-bent). Then we played with the bent top piece again in the side tables, adding the free-form inlay that is picked up in the standing mirror. Remember, "Always Improve."

In this project, as with all our commissions, we designed these pieces to a budget. (There's that list again: "Be Smart with Money.") I know that many readers would like to know what that budget was, so here goes: In two installments over the course of a year (while producing other work), our shop put more than 450 hours into this project. Go ahead and insert your own labor rate, overhead, and materials. And remember, "Keep Working!"

CURT WESSEL

A Simple Table in Elm

MADE FOR A SINGLE PURPOSE. The owners of Gills Rock Stoneware in Naples, Florida, wanted a small table to display a single piece of pottery in their gallery. The author responded with this table in elm, which complements rather than over-whelms the pottery.

Things get hectic during the summer and fall in Door County, Wisconsin, where I live. Tourists love the area, and my custom furniture business is usually busy at that time of year. So I didn't have much time to spare when Judy and Larry Thoreson asked me to build a small table for their Florida pottery gallery. Although I didn't want a complicated design, I did want a table that would look elegant in a fine gallery.

With this table, I designed as I built rather than draw things out. This process usually works for me on smaller pieces of furniture. My wife, Beth, suggested that I add some curvature to the legs, and I liked the idea. That was my design starting point. I wanted a delicate look, so I just started at the bandsaw with some scrap and began experimenting. I liked the broad bevel on the outside corner of the leg, and I matched the outward curve at the bottom of the leg with the same shape on the inside corner, so the bottom of the leg sweeps outward slightly.

Simplicity for the apron design meant no complicated edge treatments or moldings—just a curve to provide some visual interest. I used biscuit joints to attach the legs to the aprons, and I reinforced the joints with corner blocks inside. I used traditional joinery where it's needed, but the table is small and will be looked at more than it's used. No one will be kneading dough on it.

For the top I chose wood with nice, straight grain, all from the same plank. The top is screwed to the aprons, and the holes through the top are slotted to allow for seasonal wood movement. Instead of plugging the screw holes with a typical end-grain plug, I used diamond-shaped purpleheart plugs.

LINES ARE SIMPLE AND EFFECTIVE. A wide chamfer on the outside of the legs and a delicate curve on the bottom edges of the aprons make up the only ornamentation the table needed.

A DIAMOND, NOT A SQUARE. Diamond-shaped purpleheart plugs cover the screws that attach the top to the table aprons.

SPECIFICATIONS

- DIMENSIONS
  28 in. long, 12 in. wide, and 28 in. high

- MATERIALS
  Elm and purpleheart

- FINISH
  Tung oil and paste wax

PETER BARRETT

Lacewood
Stereo Cabinet

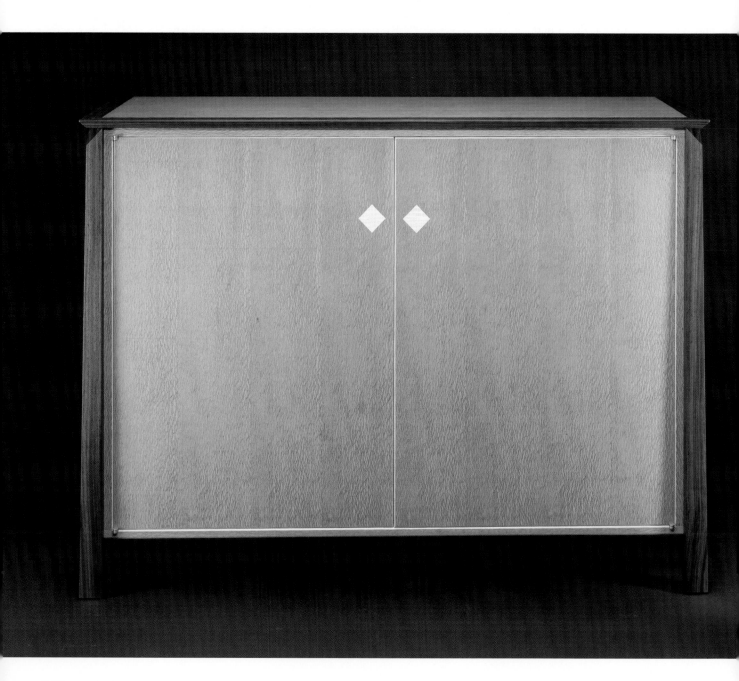

Medieval and modern architectural references were among the things on my mind as I designed this cabinet. I came to furniture from a background in building, both driving nails and drawing plans, so I suppose all my furniture comes through architecture.

The leg design has a hint of a medieval cathedral in it. I've always liked the buttress—a vertical spine jutting out from a wall to brace it—as an appealing expression of a building's structure. I designed the legs of this cabinet so they'd stand out from the carcase in a similar way. Cathedral buttresses were often angled at the top to shed water, and I've picked up that detail here, making the legs seem even more distinct from the body of the cabinet. I amplified the effect by using an undercut bevel on the rosewood edge of the top.

Still, I doubt that this piece is going to remind anyone of a medieval cathedral. Maybe that's because I'm most at home with the minimalism and planar geometry of International Style architecture, and those ideas are at the heart of most of my furniture designs.

Structural honesty is one attribute that links the medieval with the modern, and I try to design so the details express the structure of a piece. With this cabinet, in addition to having the legs distinct from the case, I gave the doors a small chamfer around the perimeter. The chamfer cuts right through the lacewood veneer to the maple banding. I hoped this would lighten the piece, emphasize the flatness of the surface, and be a reminder that it's veneered.

ROSEWOOD GEMSTONE. The author's interest in jewelry is reflected in the faceted and polished rosewood surfaces.

SPECIFICATIONS

- **DIMENSIONS**
  48 in. long, 18 in. wide, and 30 in. high

- **MATERIALS**
  Mahogany, mahogany veneer plywood, and ebonized mahogany

- **FINISH**
  Aniline dye, wiping stain, and catalyzed lacquer

BUILDING BLOCKS. Architectural influences from medieval churches and the International Style come together in this lacewood and rosewood cabinet.

JAMES PROBST

Contemporary Cherry Credenza

CLEAN, CONTEMPORARY LINES. The author used cherry left over from another project, along with two kinds of maple, to build this simple design. The basic rectilinear shape is softened with subtle curves.

DETAILS COMPLEMENT EACH OTHER. This cabinet uses curves on the case's sides, the bottom rail, and the edge of the top, and also in the butterfly-wing shapes of the door and drawer pulls.

To take a break from my full-time, production furniture making, I sometimes need to design and build a piece just for the fun of it. That was the motivation for my credenza. I wanted a cabinet with curved sides, but I also wanted to keep the lines clean, subtle, and uncluttered. I had some 8/4 cherry left over from a conference-table project and was able to get the curve I wanted for the sides by bandsawing it into one face of the stock.

I wanted the curve to carry itself around the piece, so I added a cove cut to the underside of the ends of the top. In my drawings for the piece, I continued this detail by sketching a curve to the bottom of the lower rail. However, the final line of the curve was ultimately dictated by the grain of the wood I used. The door pulls are made from the wane of the curly maple boards from the door panels. The pull faces have a pebblelike texture, which I felt added

a nice contrast to the smooth finish of the rest of the cabinet. The inspiration for their shape came from butterfly wings. I repeated the shape in the cutouts for the drawer pulls inside. The use of the curly maple for the door panels, while adding visual contrast to the piece, also tended to emphasize the perimeter lines of the cabinet.

SPECIFICATIONS

■ DIMENSIONS
42 in. wide, 20 in. deep, and 30 in. high

■ MATERIALS
Cherry, curly maple, and hard maple

■ FINISH
Tung oil and urethane mixture and paste wax

JOHN CAMERON

Pearwood Cabinet on Stand

AN APPEALING SHOWCASE. The convex doors, when open, continue the curve of the inside drawers. The darker-wood stand anchors the cabinet to the floor.

SPECIFICATIONS

■ DIMENSIONS
14¾ in. wide, 11 in. deep, and 43 in. high

■ MATERIALS
Swiss pearwood

■ FINISH
Thinned shellac and wax

When I was visiting the period rooms in the Boston Museum of Fine Arts, I was intrigued by a small chest on a stand in a Louis XV display. While the overly ornate styling did nothing for me, the unique size of the piece drew me in. It was small for a cabinet but large for a jewelry chest. It stood out on its own in the center of the room.

My cabinet of Swiss pearwood loosely reinterpreted the period piece but in a modern light. It looks nothing like the museum piece, but it retains the odd size—not too big and not too small. I also made both the front and the rear convex to allow the cabinet to stand away from a wall, if desired.

The upper cabinet was made from a calm, light-in-color plank that I felt would look great in a piece with smooth, clean lines. The interior is uncluttered, with a gallery of two drawers running in a concave arc along the bottom of the case. The stand was made from the darkest pear I could find to contrast with the top and to hold it firmly to the ground.

PETER BARRETT is a furniture designer. He studied architectural design and worked as a residential architect before he began to build furniture.

E. E. "SKIP" BENSON is a custom furniture maker and sculptor in Camden, Maine. A graduate of the master woodworker's program at the Rochester Institute of Technology, he designed and taught the woodworking program for the California College of Arts and Crafts in Oakland from 1977 to 1985.

JOHN BURCHETT is a custom furniture maker in Copnor, Portsmouth, England.

JOHN CAMERON has been a musician and cabinetmaker for most of his adult life. He studied at the College of the Redwoods with James Krenov and now works and teaches in Boston, Massachusetts.

ROSS DAY builds custom furniture in Poulsbo, Washington, and teaches furniture making part-time at the community-college level. His work has been featured in various shows and publications.

DAVID FAY designs and builds custom furniture in Oakland, California. His work has been featured in *Fine Woodworking, Home Furniture, Woodworker West,* and *The New York Times.*

CHARLES GRIVAS is a graduate of the North Bennett School. With 20 years' experience in woodworking, he specializes in Shaker-style furniture in West Cornwall, Connecticut.

PAUL HARRELL studied at the College of the Redwoods and is now a furniture maker in Pittsboro, North Carolina.

MICHAEL HURWITZ is an award-winning furniture maker in Philadelphia, Pennsylvania. His work has been included in numerous exhibitions and museums.

SETH JANOFSKY is a furniture craftsman in Fort Bragg, California, who exhibits widely.

CHARLES E. JOHNSON graduated from college and began his own company installing architectural millwork and building stairs. He founded the Contemporary Furniture Studio in Farmington, New Mexico, in 1993.

DARRYL KEIL owns and operates Vacuum Pressing Systems in Brunswick, Maine. He also teaches classes on veneering at the Center for Furniture Craftsmanship in Rockport, Maine.

PETER KORN makes furniture and teaches woodworking at the Center for Furniture Craftsmanship in Rockland, Maine. He is the author of *Working with Wood: The Basics of Craftsmanship* and *The Woodworkers' Guide to Hand Tools* (The Taunton Press).

M. FELIX MARTI is a designer and builder in Ridgway, Colorado.

GENE MARTIN has been designing and building custom homes and furniture for over 20 years. He recently built a timber-frame workshop beside his home in Innerkip, Ontario.

GARY NAKAMOTO has been working with wood for 10 years. He is the creator of interactive sculptures that use wood as the primary medium.

DARRELL PEART has been a professional woodworker since 1970. He builds custom furniture in the Puget Sound area.

PHILIP PONVERT is a furniture designer and master craftsman living in Sedona, Arizona.

JAMES PROBST is a self-taught woodworker who runs a two-person shop that primarily makes Shaker-influenced casework and tables.

MASON RAPAPORT designs and builds furniture in Easthampton, Massachusetts. His work has been included in over 40 shows and numerous newspaper, magazine, and book articles. Most recently he was featured in *Modern Masters* on HGTV.

GARY ROGOWSKI designs and builds custom furniture and teaches woodworking at the Oregon School of Arts and Crafts in Portland, Oregon. He is a contributing editor for *Fine Woodworking* magazine and the author of *The Complete Illustrated Guide to Joinery* (The Taunton Press).

LINDSAY SUTER is a woodworker and architect in North Branford, Connecticut. He has taught at the California College of Arts and Crafts in Oakland, California, and Yale University in New Haven, Connecticut.

PETER TURNER builds custom furniture in Portland, Maine. His work has been featured in exhibitions, magazines, and books. He teaches at The Center for Furniture Craftsmanship in Rockport, Maine.

DAVID TUTTLE is studying pastoral care near Winnipeg, Manitoba. He also runs a furniture-making and repair shop.

PATRICK WARNER has 30 years' experience making jigs, fixtures, and furniture and is the manufacturer of the Warner router base. He has written numerous books and articles on routing, including *The Router Book* (The Taunton Press).

CURT WESSEL is a self-taught furniture maker and cabinetmaker in Door County, Wisconsin. He teaches woodworking at The Clearing, a folk school founded by Jens Jensen, a landscape architect.

CREDITS

The articles compiled in this book appeared in the following issues of *Fine Woodworking (FWW)* and *Home Furniture (HF)*:

p. 6: Table and Chairs with a Split Personality by E. E. "Skip" Benson, *HF* issue 13. Photos by Jonathan Binzen, © The Taunton Press, Inc.

p. 10: A Stylish Credenza by Patrick Warner, *FWW* issue 105. Photos © Kevin Halle. Illustration by David Dann, © The Taunton Press, Inc.

p. 16: Extraordinary Built-ins by Ross Day, *FWW* issue 149. Photos by Anatole Burkin, © The Taunton Press, Inc. Illustration by Michael Gellatly, © The Taunton Press, Inc.

p. 26: Component-Built Sideboard by Seth Janofsky, *FWW* issue 137. Photos on pp. 26, 30, 32 (top, bottom right), 33 (bottom), 34, 35, 36 (top right), and 37 (bottom center, bottom right) © Seth Janofsky; pp. 28, 29, 31, 32 (bottom left), 33 (top), 36 (top left, bottom left, bottom right), and 37 (top left, top center, top right, bottom left) by Jonathan Binzen, © The Taunton Press, Inc. Illustrations on pp. 26 and 33 by Seth Janofsky, © The Taunton Press, Inc.; pp. 27 and 34 by Bob La Pointe, © The Taunton Press, Inc.

p. 38: Build a Harvest Table by Gary Rogowski, *FWW* issue 112. Photos by Vincent Laurence, © The Taunton Press, Inc. Illustration by Maria Meleschnig, © The Taunton Press, Inc.

p. 44: Knockdown Computer Desk by David Tuttle, *FWW* issue 103. Photos by Alec Waters, © The Taunton Press, Inc. Illustrations by Heather Lambert, © The Taunton Press, Inc.

p. 50: Building an Open-Pedestal Table by John Burchett, *FWW* issue 109. Photos © John Burchett. Illustrations by Bob La Pointe, © The Taunton Press, Inc.

p. 56: Frame-and-Panel Bed by David Fay, *FWW* issue 134. Photos on p. 56 © Ira Schrank; pp. 57, 60, 62, and 64 by Anatole Burkin, © The Taunton Press, Inc. Illllustrations by Vince Babak, © The Taunton Press, Inc.

p. 65: Mahogany Bedside Table by Charles Grivas, *FWW* issue 131. Photos on pp. 65 and 67 © Andre Baranowski; pp. 68 and 70–72 by Jefferson Kolle, © The Taunton Press, Inc. Illustrations by Bob La Pointe, © The Taunton Press, Inc.

p. 73: Curved Panels from a Vacuum Veneer Press by Mason Rapaport, *FWW* issue 110. Photos on p. 73 by Robert Marsala, © The Taunton Press, Inc.; pp. 74–77 by Vincent Laurence, © The Taunton Press, Inc.

p. 78: A Hall Table That's Both Traditional and Contemporary by Peter Korn, *FWW* issue 113. Photos on pp. 78–79 © Kip Brundage; p. 80 by Vincent Laurence, © The Taunton Press, Inc. Illustrations by Bob La Pointe, © The Taunton Press, Inc.

p. 84: Entertainment Center in Quartersawn Maple by Peter Turner, *FWW* issue 139. Photos by Anatole Burkin, © The Taunton Press, Inc. Illustrations by Bob La Pointe, © The Taunton Press, Inc.

p. 96: Joinery for Light, Sturdy Coffee Table by Lindsay Suter, *FWW* issue 114. Photos by Charley Robinson, © The Taunton Press, Inc. Illustrations by Michael Gellatly, © The Taunton Press, Inc.

p. 102: Shelving, Plain and Simple by M. Felix Marti, *FWW* issue 113. Photos on p. 102 © M. Felix Marti; p. 105 by Alec Waters, © The Taunton Press, Inc. Illustrations by Kathleen Rushton, © The Taunton Press, Inc.

p. 106: Gate-Leg Table Is Light but Sturdy by Gary Rogowski, *FWW* issue 108. Photos on pp. 107, 108, 112, and 113 by Vincent Laurence, © The Taunton Press, Inc.; p. 109 © Jim Piper. Illustrations by Heather Lambert, © The Taunton Press, Inc.

p. 114: Using Shop-Sawn Veneer by Paul Harrell, *FWW* issue 107. Photos on p. 115 © Sloan Howard; pp. 117–119 by Jonathan Binzen, © The Taunton Press, Inc. Illustrations by Bob La Pointe, © The Taunton Press, Inc.

p. 124: Strategies for Curved Work by Darryl Keil, *FWW* issue 139. Photos on p. 124 (bottom) courtesy Darryl Keil; pp. 124 (top) and 126–133 by Anatole Burkin, © The Taunton Press, Inc. Illustrations by Vince Babak, © The Taunton Press, Inc.

p. 136: Dining Set in Cherry and Imbuya by Gene Martin, *HF* issue 3. Photos by Zachary Gaulkin, © The Taunton Press, Inc.

p. 138: Audio Cabinet in Cherry and Wenge by Darrell Peart, *HF* issue 2. Photos © Jeff Zagun. Illustration © Kathleen Rushton.

p. 142: Lacewood Writing Desk by Charles E. Johnson, *HF* issue 2. Photos © Diane Davis.

p. 144: Cloud Rise Bed by Gary Rogowski, *HF* issue 8. Photos on pp. 144–145 by Zachary Gaulkin, © The Taunton Press, Inc.; p. 146 (top) © Harold Wood; p. 146 (bottom) © Phil Harris.

p. 147: Fresh Curves for a Kitchen Table by Michael Hurwitz, *HF* issue 11. Photos by Jonathan Binzen, © The Taunton Press, Inc.

p. 150: A Bent-Plywood Chair Built for Good Posture by Gary Nakamoto, *HF* issue 12. Photos by Zachary Gaulkin, © The Taunton Press, Inc. Location courtesy Misugi Design, Berkeley, Calif.

p. 153: Circles, Inlays and Curves Unite a Bedroom Suite by Philip Ponvert, *HF* issue 10. Photo by Zachary Gaulkin, © The Taunton Press, Inc. Illustrations © Philip Ponvert.

p. 156: A Simple Table in Elm by Curt Wessel, *HF* issue 4. Photos by Scott Gibson, © The Taunton Press, Inc.

p. 158: Lacewood Stereo Cabinet by Peter Barrett, *HF* issue 7. Photos © Stretch Tuemmler.

p. 160: Contemporary Cherry Credenza by James Probst, *HF* issue 9. Photos © Michael Keller.

p. 162: Pearwood Cabinet on Stand by John Cameron, *HF* issue 4. Photos © David Welter.

Front matter photo credits:

p. ii: © Kevin Halle (left); Jonathan Binzen, © The Taunton Press, Inc. (center); © Diane Davis (right).

p. iii: Robert Marsala, © The Taunton Press, Inc.

p. vi: Anatole Burkin, © The Taunton Press, Inc.

p. 1: Alec Waters, © The Taunton Press, Inc. (top left); Jonathan Binzen, © The Taunton Press, Inc. (top right); courtesy Darryl Keil (bottom).

p. 2: © Kip Brundage.

Section openers photo credits:

p. 4: Jonathan Binzen, © The Taunton Press, Inc. (left); Anatole Burkin, © The Taunton Press, Inc. (center and right).

p. 5: Anatole Burkin, © The Taunton Press, Inc.

p. 24: Anatole Burkin, © The Taunton Press, Inc. (left and right); Alec Waters, © The Taunton Press, Inc. (center).

p. 25: Anatole Burkin, © The Taunton Press, Inc.

p. 134: © Stretch Tuemmler (left); Zachary Gaulkin, © The Taunton Press, Inc., location courtesy Misugi Design, Berkeley, Calif. (center); Jonathan Binzen, © The Taunton Press, Inc.

p. 135: Scott Gibson, © The Taunton Press, Inc.

Cover photo credits:

front: courtesy Darryl Keil (large); © Michael Keller (inset left); Vincent Laurence, © The Taunton Press, Inc. (inset center); Jonathan Binzen, © The Taunton Press, Inc. (inset right).

back: © Kevin Halle (large); © Michael Keller (inset left); © Bill Arsenault (inset center); Anatole Burkin, © The Taunton Press, Inc. (inset right).

spine: Anatole Burkin, © The Taunton Press, Inc.

Note: page references in italics indicate a photograph; references in bold indicate a drawing.

A

Audio cabinet in cherry and wenge:
    base design and construction, 140, ***140***
    exposed joinery of, 138, *138*
    storage and easy-access back, *141*

B

Barrett, Peter, 158-59
Bed, cloud rise form in, *144*, 145, *145*, 146, *146*
Bed, frame-and-panel:
    adding inlay contrast, 62, *62*, 64
    cleaning up the posts, 61
    components and assembly of, **58**
    cutting the joinery, 57, *57*, 59
    establishing the outside curves, 57
    finishing with hand-rubbed oil, 64
    frame compatibility options, 63, 65
    grinding the facets, 57
    making a hidden bed-rail-to-post connection, 63, **63**
    routing curved templates, 60, *60*
    shaping the bedposts, *57*
    six-sided headboard and footboard, 61
Bedroom suite, circles, inlays, and curves in, 153, *153*, **154**, 155
Bedside tables:
    in bedroom suite, 153, *153*, **154**, 155
    mahogany bedside table, 65–72
Benson, E. E. "Skip", 6–9
Bent-plywood chairs, *150*, 151, *151*, 152, *152*
Built-ins with modern style and design:
    cabinetmaking skills and, 22, **23**
    designing for a bedroom, 16, *16*, 17, 18, *18*
    fitting and installing, 22, **23**
    joinery in, 19, *19*
    quality materials for, 18, *18*, 19
    refining details in, 19, *22*, 22
Burchett, John, 50–55

C

Cameron, John, 162–63
Chairs:
    bent-plywood chairs, *150*, 151, *151*, 152, *152*
    dining set in cherry and imbuya, *136*, 137, *137*
    in softened four-square format, 6, 7, *7*, *8*, 9, *9*
Chinese design influences, *144*, 145–46
Coffee table, joinery for:
    assembling the frame in two steps, 99, *99*
    components of, **98**
    cutting mortises with a dado blade, 97, *97*
    laying out stretchers from the legs, 98
    making butterfly joints, 99, *99*, 100
    tenoned, mortised, and tapered legs, 97–98
    wedged through-tenons, **101**
Computer desk, knockdown version of:
    assembly and wiring, 48–49
    components and assembly of, **45**
    constructing the desk, 47, *47*, 48, *48*, 49, *49*
    CPU cabinet in, 44, *44*, **45**, 46, **46**
    edge-banding and solid trim, 47, *47*
    flip-up keyboard tray extension, **46**
    making shopmade threaded inserts, 48, *48*, 49, *49*
    making the door and prefinishing parts, 48
    routing openings and installing inserts, 47–48, *48*
    wiring the CPU cabinet, 46, **46**
Credenza, contemporary lines in cherry, *160*, 161, *161*
Credenza, modern style and design in:
    details in, 14–15, *15*
    joinery in, 12, *12*, **13**, 14
    "no finish" finish in, 11, *11*
    options and adaptations, 11–12

Curved panels from a vacuum veneer press:
    drying with an electric blanket, 77
    gluing, 76, *76*
    inside the vacuum bag, 76–77
    making the form, 74, *74*, *75*
    preparing substrate and the veneer, 75, *75*

D

Day, Ross, 16–23
Desks:
    knockdown computer desk, 44–49
    lacewood writing desk, *142*, 143, *143*
Dining set in cherry and imbuya, *136*, 137, *137*

E

Entertainment center:
    assembly of frame-and-panel base, **86**
    assembly of upper case, **93**
    building the dovetailed upper case, 92, *92*, 93, **93**
    building the lower case, 87, *87*
    crown molding for, 89, *89*, 94
    hardware for, 94, *95*
    making drawers and drawer slides, 90–91, *91*
    measuring for electronic components, 84, *85*
    in quartersawn maple, 84–95
    waist molding for, 88, *88*, 90

F

Fay, David, 56–64
Finishes:
    ebonized wood, 83
    milk paint finish, 41, 43
    "no finish" finish, 11, *11*
    See also specific project
Ford, Malcolm, 48

G

Gate-leg table:
    accurate mortising fixture, **111**, 112, *112*
    components and assembly of, **110**
    cutting overlong brushings, 108, *108*, 109
    fitting the gates, *107*, 109, 110, 111
    gluing sequence in, 109
    joinery and pivots in, 106, *107*, 108, *108*, 109
    making the oval tabletop, 113
    using a table-saw tenoning jig, **111**, 112, *112*
Grain, in softened four-square format, *8, 9*
Grew-Sheridan, Carolyn, 151, 152
Grew-Sheridan, John, 151, 152
Grivas, Charles, 65–72

H

Hall table:
    building the base, 79, **79**, 81
    components and assembly of, **81**
    finishing, 83
    gluing up the parts, **82**
    making half-lap joints, *80*
    making the top, 81
    planing, scraping, and sanding, 83
    table joinery in, **82**
Harrell, Paul, 114–23
Harvest table:
    finishing the base and pegging the tenons, *38*, 41, 43, *43*
    gluing up in sections, 40–41, *41*
    making and fitting tenon stock, *39*, 40
    making, finishing, and attaching the top, 43, *43*
    mortising legs and rails, 39, *39*, 40
    preparing for a finish with a hand-plane, *39*, 40
    tapering the legs, 39
    taper jig, making and using, 42, **42**, *43*
Heitzman, Roger, 73
Hurwitz, Michael, 147–49

I

Inspiration:
    circles, inlays, and curves in a bedroom suite, 153, *153*, **154**, 155
    cloud rise bed, *144*, 145, *145, 146*
    contemporary cherry credenza, *160*, 161, *161*
    fresh curves in a kitchen table, 147, *147*, 148, *148, 149*
    simple table in elm, 156, 157, *157*
    See also Wood/woods
    See also specific project

J

Janofsky, Seth, 26–37
Japanese design influences, 16, 28, 35, 145
Jigs:
    making and using a taper jig, 42, **42**, *43*
    using a table-saw tenoning jig, **111**, 112, *112*
Johnson, Charles E., 142–43

K

Keil, Darryl, 124–33
Kitchen table, fresh curves in:
    crisscrossing veneer strips in the tabletop, 148, *148*
    footroom under, 147, *147*, 148, *149*
Korn, Peter, 78–83
Krenov, James, 138, *139*

L

Lacewood stereo cabinet:
    faceted and polished rosewood surfaces, *159*
    medieval and modern references in, *158*, 159, *159*
Lacewood writing desk, *142*, 143, *143*
Laine, Mike, 63

M

Mackintosh, Charles Rennie, 145
Mahogany bedside table:
    components and assembly of, **66**
    cutting and marking the legs, 67, *68*, 69
    cutting biscuits after tapering two sides, *68*, 69
    detailing the top, 71–72, *72*
    dry-fitting the case, 69, *70*, 71
    marking for the top, shelf, and bottom, 69, *70*, 71
    octagon-shaped legs, 65, *65*, 67, *67*, *68*, 69
    using edge-banding tape in construction, 71, *71*
Marti, M. Felix, 102–5
Martin, Gene, 136–37

N

Nakamoto, Gary, 150–52

O

Open-pedestal table:
    assembly procedure, **51**, *52*, 54, *54*, 55
    cutting the joints, 53, *53*, 54
    finishing up, 55
    gluing up the top, 55
    open framework of, 50, *50*
    working with templates, 52, **52**, 53

P

Peart, Darrell, 138–41
Pearwood cabinet on a stand, 162, *162*, *163*
Philadelphia Furniture Show, 84, 94
Ponvert, Philip, 153–55
Probst, James, 160–61

R

Rapaport, Mason, 73–77
Rietveld, Gerrit, 7
Rogowski, Gary, 38–43, 106–13, 144–46

S

Scandinavian design influences, 28
Shelving:
    assembling shelves and uprights,
        103, 105, **105**
    cutting the stock to size, 103
    laminating shelf stock, 103
    making a knockdown version, 105
    using a dado for corner uprights,
        103, *103*, **104**
    using different materials, 105
Sideboard, component-built:
    applying finish before glue-up, 32,
        32, 33
    constructing the base, **27**, 33, *33*
    designing, 26, *26*, **27**, 28–29
    doweling in, 30, *30*, 31, *31*, 32
    installing adjustable shelves, 35, *35*
    legs and sides as a unit, *28*, 29, *29*,
        30
    sliding drawers and drawer boxes,
        34, 35, *36–37*
Sideboard, from shop-sawn veneer:
    components and assembly of,
        120–21
    core materials for, 119, 122
    creating a pattern with sawn veneer,
        117, *117*
    edge-joining veneers, 118–19, *119*
    edging options for veneered panels,
        122
    finding a bandsaw blade's natural
        cutting angle, 116, **118**
    laying out a plank, 116, **116**
    preparing for the press, 122, **122,**
        123
    sawing veneer, 116, **118**
    shooting the veneer edges, 119, *119*
    structural advantages of veneered
        panels, **120–21**
    using a clamp-and-caul veneer press,
        123, **123**
    veneer vs. solid wood, 114
    wedge-gluing the veneer edge joints,
        119, *119*

Simple table in elm:
    designing with building, 157
    diamond-shaped purpleheart plugs,
        157, *157*
Suter, Lindsay, 96–101

T

Tables:
    dining set in cherry and imbuya,
        136, 137, *137*
    gate-leg table, 106–13
    hall table, 78–83
    harvest table, 38–43
    kitchen table, fresh curves in,
        147–49
    mahogany bedside table, 65–72
    open-pedestal table, 50–55
    simple table in elm, *156*, 157, *157*
    in softened four-square format, *6,*
        7–9
Turner, Peter, 84–95
Tuttle, David, 44–49

V

Vacuum veneer press, curved panels
    from:
    drying with an electric blanket, 77
    gluing, 76, *76*
    inside the vacuum bag, 76–77, *77*
    making the form, 74, *74*, 75
    preparing substrate and the veneer,
        75, *75*
Vacuum veneer press, strategies for
    curved work:
    choosing the right glue, 132, *132*
    core materials for curved work, **130**
    designing the piece and dimensions
        of the form, 125–26, *126*,
        127
    edge-banding goes on last, 130,
        133, *133*
    gluing two-ply veneers onto the
        core, **128**, 129, *129*, 130
    making forms rigid in the right
        places, 125, **125**, 126, *126*,
        127

preparing the core, 127, **128**, 129
sizing parts for typical forms and
    cores, **125**
trimming the finished piece, 130,
    130
veneering the sides, **130**
Veneer:
    crisscrossing veneer strips in a table-
        top, 148, *148*
    sideboard from shop-sawn veneer,
        114–23
    veneered curves with a vacuum
        veneer press, 73–77

W

Warner, Patrick, 10–15
Wessel, Curt, 156–57
Wood/woods:
    American walnut, *50, 52, 53, 54*
    audio cabinet in cherry and wenge,
        138–41
    birch veneer computer desk, 44–49
    cherry gate-leg table, *107, 108, 109*
    cherry hall table, *78, 79, 80*
    cocobolo accents, *142,* 143, *143*
    contemporary cherry credenza, *160,*
        161, *161*
    credenza in yellow satinwood and
        maple, *10, 11, 12, 15*
    dining set in cherry and imbuya,
        136, 137, *137*
    jarrah veneer, *115, 117, 118, 119*
    lacewood stereo cabinet, *158*, 159,
        159
    lacewood writing desk, *142*, 143,
        143
    mahogany sideboard, *115*
    pearwood cabinet on stand, 162,
        162, 163
    quartersawn maple, 84–95
    simple table in elm, *156*, 157, *157*
    types in a frame-and-panel bed, *56,*
        56
    white oak sideboard, 26–37
    See also specific project